LEADING
FOR *freedom*
Leadership Skills for Republicans

RACHEL WOODS & TONI ANNE DASHIELL
FOREWORD BY U.S. SENATOR JOHN CORNYN

LEADING FOR FREEDOM
Leadership Skills for Republicans

Copyright © 2012 by Woods & Dashiell Consulting, LLC

Published by PCG Legacy
a division of Pilot Communications Group, Inc.

All names used in the stories in *Leading for Freedom: Leadership Skills for Republicans* are fictitious. Any resemblance to real persons, living or deceased, is purely coincidental.

Cover design by Neue Creative
Photography by Ann E. Harrington

ISBN 978-1-936417-78-0

Printed in the United States of America

To reach the authors:
www.leading4freedom.com

Dedicated
to Tom, Riley, Jackson, and Reagan

WHAT REPUBLICAN LEADERS ARE SAYING ABOUT *LEADING FOR FREEDOM*

"Our democracy requires strong leadership, both at the national level in Washington and at the grassroots level in towns and cities across the country. That's why this book is so important. Rachel and Toni Anne show they have thought long and hard about the most effective ways to advance our shared conservative principles. *Leading for Freedom* provides sound advice for elected leaders and private citizens hoping to make a difference."
— *U.S. Senator John Cornyn*

"Today many who are elected or work in political parties think a leader is someone who watches which way the band is marching and runs to get in front. Not only are such people not leaders, they are the worst kind of followers. Rachel and Toni Anne do an amazing job of not only teaching about true leaders, but also disclosing how to become a leader or become a better one in very concise steps. They also utilize factual examples that indelibly etch the lessons in our minds. This is an invaluable resource."
— *U.S. Congressman Louie Gohmert*

"*Leading for Freedom* is a timeless resource for grassroots Republicans."
— *U.S. Congressman Lamar Smith*

"Texas has established a strong model of conservative leadership for the nation to follow. *Leading for Freedom* is a roadmap to continue on our journey by educating the leaders of tomorrow.

Rachel and Toni Anne have done a great job of laying out a clear and crisp blueprint for Republicans. I commend them for their fine work."
— *Susan Combs, Texas Comptroller*

"*Leading for Freedom* is a great treatise on small unit leadership that is the base and foundation of our party. Most of all, as Rachel and Toni Anne teach the skills of effective leadership, they also inherently teach the most important trait for future leaders, and that is to first be a good follower."
— *Lt Col (Ret) U.S. Army/Texas State Senator, Brian Birdwell*

"Some talk the talk, but fail to walk the walk. Dashiell and Woods put on paper how to do both and win!"
— *Luke Marchant, Former Political Director for Sen. Marco Rubio*

"I am just thrilled to be able to endorse this book written by Toni Anne Dashiell and Rachel Woods. Their expertise and knowledge of the political process, training candidates and implementation of the "how to" plans for success has proven to be valuable at both local, state and national levels of government. Easy to understand with real life examples of TEAM building make this book a must read for everyone wanting to participate in the political process. Two women with great leadership skills — sharing their ideas to make a difference for a better America!"
— *Sue Lynch, Past President National Federation of Republican Women*

"Four Stars! *Leading for Freedom* is sure to be an instant classic among Republican activists."
— *Melinda Fredricks, Vice-Chairman Republican Party of Texas*

"Republican leaders, Woods and Dashiell, have drafted a straightforward book which acts as a colorful atlas showing us the smart route in our quest to winning elections."
— *Elizabeth "Besa" Martin, Vice-President of Legislation Texas Federation of Republican Women*

PREFACE

Freedom is under attack in our country, not just by our enemies but by our very own leaders who, by their actions, seek to destroy the foundation upon which this nation was founded. These leaders believe that government is the answer, but their policies ultimately disempower the very people they profess to represent. We do not believe that government is the answer. We believe it is the problem.

We believe in freedom. Freedom from government-run healthcare. Freedom from Washington bureaucrats making decisions about our children's educations, freedom from high taxation, freedom from high government regulation stifling our business's growth. But who stands for freedom in this country? Which party strives to limit the reach of our ever increasing government?

The Republican Party is today and historically the party of freedom. We are the party of Abraham Lincoln and Ronald Reagan, who gave us the Emancipation Proclamation and brought down the Berlin Wall, respectively.

We are grassroots political activists who have spent countless hours supporting candidates and causes of the Republican Party. Our experience working in numerous Republican organizations, including campaigns, the Republican Party and auxiliary organizations, have introduced us to people, both paid and volunteer, who understand what is at stake in our country. They work many hours, tirelessly — all in the name of freedom.

You understand this community of patriots that we describe, because you are part of it. We are not abroad on the front lines in a battle zone, but nonetheless, we are fighting. We are fighting with our money, our influence, our time and talent to preserve freedom in this country. We are fighting for a United States that we can proudly pass on to our children.

Also, like you, we have found ourselves wishing we could do something more. Something to help Republicans succeed in their mission.... Something. Because, despite our best efforts, there is still a sinking feeling that the America we know is slipping from our grasp, and before too long it may be beyond our reach. So we asked ourselves, "What more can we do?" For us, the answer to this question is one that we are very passionate about. The answer is one which has the potential to draw out the best in us. The answer can help us to more effectively and efficiently accomplish the missions of the Republican organizations that we know and serve. The answer we found is leadership development. Leadership development is not the answer to everything, of course, but it is certainly a large piece of the puzzle; one for which each of us can be personally accountable.

Why did we come to this conclusion? We both share insight into the world of leadership development and also Republican politics. We have trained leaders from across the United States and from six different countries to date. We understand the value of leadership development. We see its potential to transform people and organizations. We have seen it work in our own lives and organizations as we continue to grow and develop in our own leadership skills.

It is because of this perspective that we see leadership development as an untapped strategic opportunity for the Republican Party. What we see and what we want every Republican to see is that there is a connection between a leader's actions and an organization's results. Years of research and an entire leadership development industry confirm this.

It works in the business world, so why not apply the same principles to our political organizations? What we know to be true is that between a plan of action and the action itself is a gap. In that gap is the leader. It is the leader's skill set that closes or does not close that gap. If a plan of action is given to two people, two different outcomes will result. In other words, how a plan of action is executed matters just as much as having a plan of action itself.

And while it seems impossible and even utopian to think that the Republican Party can develop in ways that traditional organizations do, because of the numerous independent Republican organizations that exist, it is certainly possible for us to share our message with individual Republicans who share our vision. After all, the choice to set goals and reach them is deeply personal. Therefore, if we inspire only one person to develop skills that help him or her run a Republican organization better or to see a project through to its completion, then our efforts will be worthwhile. However, our vision is to inspire a Party, a movement of grassroots Republicans who see the value in our individual and combined efforts.

Our ultimate purpose is to inspire, challenge and equip Republicans with leadership development tools that will help us all become better leaders. We do not wish for Republicans to work harder or longer, but more efficiently in pursuit of freedom.

Freedom is under attack in our country by leaders who think more government is the answer. We know that more *freedom* is the answer; therefore, we have work to do and not a moment to waste. We have a mission to accomplish together as a team. We have the tools and resources we need to be successful. We must utilize every opportunity we have, including leadership development, to help strengthen our team and therefore our results.

We can think of no greater purpose than for freedom.

— *Rachel Woods*
— *Toni Anne Dashiell*

FOREWORD

As the 2012 campaign heats up, we need to remember what this election is really about. It isn't really about budget arithmetic or debt-to-GDP ratios. It's about people standing up for bold free-market reform. Republicans understand that the debate over big government is not simply an economic debate; it is also a moral debate.

Our democracy requires strong leadership, both at the national level in Washington and at the grassroots level in towns and cities across the country. That's why this book is so important.

Rachel and Toni Anne show they have thought long and hard about the most effective ways to advance our shared conservative principles. *Leading for Freedom* provides sound advice for elected leaders and private citizens hoping to make a difference. The authors recognize that Republicans must do more than simply offer smart policy ideas; we must also develop the political and interpersonal skills necessary to make those ideas a reality.

To paraphrase former Supreme Court justice Potter Stewart: We can't precisely define "good leadership," but we know it when we see it. As Rachel and Toni Anne explain, good leaders tend to be good motivators, good team-builders, good delegators, good communicators, good conflict-managers, and good goal-setters. They also tend to be good at cultivating trust among friends and colleagues.

Disciplined grassroots conservative leadership has never been more important than it is today. Since 2009, we have witnessed an explosion of new federal spending and regulation. We have also experienced the weakest economic recovery since World War II.

That's not a coincidence. Washington has become a lot like the actor Errol Flynn, who famously said that he had trouble reconciling his "gross habits" with his "net income." Simply put: Unless we reverse the trend of rapid debt accumulation, we face a future of permanently reduced economic growth and a lower standard of living, a future in which programs like Medicare and Social Security may not remain viable for our children and grandchildren.

Thankfully, the 2010 elections represented a massive backlash against government overreach. In historic numbers, voters declared their opposition to Obamacare, cap-and-trade, the failed economic "stimulus" package, and other fiscally reckless policies. The message was clear: Americans want their elected officials to rediscover our Founding virtues, and they want the United States to once again become a beacon of entrepreneurial energy and robust economic growth.

Our 2010 victories have allowed Republicans to slow the Obama agenda, and they have fostered great optimism about our prospects for taming Leviathan, shrinking the national debt, and reviving the U.S. economy. Yet as the great Margaret Thatcher reminded us many years ago, "There are no permanent victories in politics," and we must not become complacent in our defense of constitutional principles. While I realize that every national election is advertised as being "the most important ever," I truly believe that 2012 could mark a watershed moment in the history of our republic, with voters choosing between two very different political philosophies.

When government becomes too large and too onerous, people grow cynical about their prospects for succeeding through hard work and personal responsibility. Their attitudes toward the welfare state and income redistribution change accordingly. Indeed, the financial meltdown and subsequent riots in Greece show us that big government can transform the character of a nation.

I support free enterprise because it is the system most conducive to human happiness. No other economic model has done more to promote a culture of aspiration and achievement. And no other economic model has done more to reduce poverty and boost living standards.

That is the message Republicans should bring to our fellow citizens. We should emphasize that the consequences of government overreach go well beyond lost jobs and crippled budgets. When Republicans fight for free enterprise, we are fighting, above all, to preserve the values that made this country so successful. We are fighting to ensure that America remains a dynamic, innovative, and upwardly mobile society.

President Obama once said that "elections have consequences." He was right, and the consequences of the 2008 election are now all too clear: runaway spending, skyrocketing debt, regulatory power grabs, and the worst economic recovery of the modern era. He has had several years to offer a credible plan for reducing long-term deficits. Not only has he failed to offer such a plan, he has rejected the bipartisan fiscal blueprint drafted by his own debt commission (the Bowles-Simpson panel).

Meanwhile, he has given us a $2.6 trillion health-care law that will exacerbate our spending crisis, raise taxes, drive up insurance costs, cause Americans to lose their existing coverage, expand an already broken Medicaid program, and allow unelected bureaucrats to make decisions that reduce patient access under Medicare.

Republicans are seeking to reverse the government excesses of the past four years and increase economic opportunity by promoting smarter tax policies, real spending cuts, lower trade barriers, and a regulatory environment that is much friendlier to job creation and investment. That is the future most Americans want, and that is the future we will strive to deliver.

But we won't succeed without a robust network of grassroots supporters. Indeed, our success will ultimately be determined, not by Republican bigwigs on K Street, but by civically engaged voters on Main Street. We need to reach beyond partisan and ideological lines to make the moral case (not just the economic case) for our principles and our policies. We need to connect with folks who normally vote Democratic or don't vote at all. We need to remember that personal interaction is a crucial component of political coalition-building. And we need to refine our message so that it carries the broadest possible appeal.

By writing this book, Rachel and Toni Anne have made a valuable contribution to our cause. I would urge all conservatives to embrace their advice and help us develop a new generation of strong leaders.

— *U.S. Senator John Cornyn, April 2012*

CONTENTS

CONFLICT MANAGEMENT

GOAL SETTING & ACTION PLANNING

APPENDIX

INTRODUCTION

Great leaders. The world is hungry for them. Once in a while we all agree that a person is an exceptionally great leader. Many Republicans agree that President Ronald Reagan was a great leader. The Reagan Era could be considered "the good ole' days" for Republicans and for Americans, particularly in lieu of the direction in which our country is headed today. To commemorate his leadership, many Republicans celebrate Reagan's birthday. It seems that he has become the face of the Republican Party. And why is this?

It is because there has been a sense of hardship and a void in leadership in our country, and people tend to think back on the past to a time when we were confident in our country's leadership. We look to Reagan during these times because we so desperately need someone like him to emerge again as a great leader of the Republican Party. But, how did Ronald Reagan become a great leader? Did he become a great leader overnight, or was he born that way?

The truth is that leadership skills can be studied and learned, but we also have to put what we learn into practice. Many people have gifts and talents that exhibit leadership potential; however, to become a great leader — requires skills that come from experience, learning, and a commitment to ongoing development. Each moment we are faced with choices that require us to make decisions. Effective decision making becomes more intuitive over time as we learn from our experiences. A key to this process is to be a life-long learner, committed to ongoing development.

Great leadership is not to be confused with perfection. Leadership is an imperfect process. Even great leaders cannot please everyone at all times. However, history judges leaders. There are people whose leadership stands the test of time. Great leaders are courageous, meaning they do the right thing even when it is not the easy option. Not only can they be decisive when a quick decision is needed, but also they can manage multiple perspectives when a situation calls for a more participative leadership style. Perhaps the most powerful quality that a leader can have is the ability to empower others. This philosophy, and the foundation of this book, is rooted in the belief that great leaders are truly servants first.

EMPOWERING OTHERS

"Empowerment" is a word that we hear often as leaders. But what is true "empowerment?" How is a leader's behavior connected to the empowerment of others and how can we empower our own members in order to strengthen the Republican Party?

"Empowerment" is the process by which leaders strengthen others in order to make them more effective. It occurs any time one person enables another to think and act with greater clarity of thought, a sense of purpose and increased courage.

The action or inaction of a leader can affect the degree of empowerment that others around them have. For example, one way a leader empowers others is through effective delegation. When we get out of the way and involve other people, we increase the ability of others to assume responsibility, make decisions and accomplish goals — and ultimately to shine!

As you will see throughout this book, leaders serve their organizations best when they provide their team members with (1) resources needed to achieve goals; and (2) support that decreases powerlessness and increases belief in themselves.

The great leader understands that no matter what our role is in an organization, we have the ability to empower each other. Each moment is an opportunity for us to empower those around us. When we selflessly empower others we demonstrate courage, confidence, character, commitment to being a team player and commitment to our cause of freedom in this country.

YOU ARE MORE POWERFUL THAN YOU KNOW

By definition leaders in organizations achieve objectives through other people. You are a leader. You may hold a formal position of leadership, you may be paid or a volunteer, but you lead every time you influence a person or group.

As a leader, you are more powerful than you know; not necessarily in the traditional ways you may think of power, but in your ability to make a lasting impact on your organization, the Republican Party. While we often recognize the significance of world leaders, we less often realize the importance of our own influence in our respective leadership roles. No matter what level of leadership you are in, there is a connection between your behavior and your organization's effectiveness.

We each have a mission that ultimately supports the goal of electing Republicans. Between the plan of action and the action itself is the specific behavior of a leader, in other words, the action that you take. The action of a leader has a great impact on whether an organization reaches its goal(s) efficiently and effectively.

If a leader tries to do everything and does not delegate, the organization will only do as much as one person is capable. The organization will be stifled by lower productivity and a less motivated worker base that does not feel a part of the organization. If a leader cannot build teams or manage varying perspectives given by team members, then the team may reach its goal more slowly than if it were led by someone who has good communication and collaboration skills.

By strengthening your leadership skills and thereby your organization's ability to accomplish its mission, you can increase the likelihood of electing Republicans. The actions you take and the decisions you make will most certainly make an impact not only on your Republican organization, but ultimately on the fabric of our country.

MAIN FEATURES OF LEADING FOR FREEDOM

The following are among the main features of *Leading for Freedom*:

- Thought-provoking questions to help you assess your current strengths and development needs.
- Short, practical chapters about essential leadership skills including:
  - Trust Building
  - Motivating Yourself and Others
  - Team Building
  - Delegating
  - Communicating
  - Managing Conflict
  - Goal-Setting
- Emphasis on Action. The content of *Leading for Freedom* is designed to help Republicans: (1) to set goals and (2) take action. Each chapter includes a section entitled "Leadership Challenge" in which we will guide you through questions that will help you apply the principles explored in the chapter to your specific leadership role or situation. Each "Leadership Challenge" will lead you to set specific goals. Additionally, we have provided you with an appendix of additional resources to assist you in your leadership development.
- Examples in *Leading for Freedom* are written in the context of multiple types of Republican organizations and apply to both volunteers and paid employees.
- Stories using fictional names and scenarios are used to exemplify leadership principles.

By picking up this book, you have expressed interest in learning how developing leadership skills can help Republicans to succeed. We now ask you to join us in our commitment to the process of leadership development, not only because it will serve you both personally and professionally, but also for the purpose of strengthening the Republican organization in the pursuit of freedom. Imagine the compounded results we can have if we are united in this commitment.

If you agree with us, please join us by signing the commitment below. Together we can make a difference.

Rachel Woods   *Toni Anne Dashiell*

I am personally committed to setting goals to develop my leadership skills for the purpose of becoming a better leader, and to strengthening the effectiveness of the Republican Party in the pursuit of freedom.

My Signature:

_____

TRUST:
A Foundation of
Leadership

The element of trust is crucial to the Republican leader. This is because leading involves having the trust of others with whom you work to achieve your Republican organization's goals. Without trust, you will be less effective and efficient in your pursuit of preserving freedoms in our country. In the following chapters we will answer these questions:

- How can you show others that you are trustworthy?
- What actions can you take to maintain or build trust?
- How can you communicate in ways that maintain or build trust?

CHAPTER 1

Trust Building

Trust is the very foundation of leadership. Leaders who do not have the trust of the people they supervise, report to, and otherwise work with cannot lead in the best sense of the word. After all, the word "leader" implies that there is a "follower," a person or group of persons who follows the leader. People sometimes manage others by virtue of their formal title, not because people truly follow them. It is certainly possible to be in a managerial role and not be considered a "leader."

In a county where there had never been a Republican chairman before, a new chairman, named Terry, was appointed and an organization was formed. This was great progress for the community and gave hope to party activists. However, after several months passed, people began to notice that Terry kept activists from volunteering in the local headquarters. Longtime, trusted volunteers stopped by the office to offer assistance — only to be turned away. Over time, people in the community grew suspicious of the leadership, wondering why only a few people were ever allowed in the office. Did they not trust the local volunteers? Did they have something to hide?

Ultimately, it did not matter why all of the secretiveness occurred. At the next election, local Republicans elected a new chair named Missie who ran on a platform of transparency and open communication. Upon her election, the office was opened up to Republican volunteers from several auxiliary Republican organizations. Missie's actions restored trust in the local Republican Party and unified the Republican community as well.

The actions we take, whether conscious or unconscious, intentional or unintentional, have an effect on others. As leaders, your actions can have an effect on whether people trust you and your organization. Because of Terry's actions, she lost the trust of the very people who wanted to help her.

The following are actions you can take that will help you to maintain trust and build credibility with others. Taking these actions will help you to not only hold a leadership *title*, but also be considered a *leader*, in the true sense of the word.

BE TRUSTWORTHY

To build trust you must first be trustworthy. Trust building begins with character and there is no substitute for this attribute. The following evidences of character can provide the basis for trust building.

- Tell the truth and earn a reputation for telling the truth.
- Never make promises you cannot or will not keep. Relate to others in such a way that they know they can trust you to do what you say you will do. The classic example of a politician making impossible campaign promises demonstrates how people can lose trust in leaders before they ever take charge.

- Commit firmly to values that respect the rights of others and the value of all people.

- Be known for doing the right thing, even when others will accept a lower standard.

- Do not let personal ambition interfere with your commitment to being honest and fair.

BE CONSISTENT IN YOUR WORDS AND ACTIONS

Does it seem as though Republicans are held to a higher standard than Democrats when it comes to moral issues? Over the years we have seen both Republican and Democratic leaders make mistakes, but we hear more about the Republican's mishaps. Why is this? One reason is because it has been Republicans that have stood up for family values and for life.

People expect leaders to be who they say they are. Once you declare who you are, people will hold you to this standard. People expect your words and deeds to be consistent with the person you profess to be. Since Republicans have professed to stand up for family values and high morals, people expect them to live it out. Does this mean that you should guard against letting people know what you believe? Absolutely not.

People must understand where leaders are coming from. This is a foundation of trust. What it means is that we must be authentic in sharing with others who we are, and must only step into positions of leadership if we know we are capable of living out these professed values. After all, it takes time to build trust and only one moment to lose it all. When you are a Republican leader, you represent more than just yourself or your family. In the eyes of others, you may be the face of the Republican Party. The consequences of your actions may only affect your neighbor's perception of Republicans or they could affect the perspective of thousands of people. A lack of trust in you can mean a lack of trust in the Republican Party.

Maintain or Build a High Level of Competence

Even when leaders are honest and trustworthy, it is possible for people to not trust their professional competence. People often expect their leaders to have experience and knowledge in the area they are managing. For example, when candidates run for president, they are held to a very high standard. Candidates are expected to have knowledge about foreign affairs, world history, economics and much more. It seems that candidates must know virtually everything these days or they are maligned by the media, even though it is impossible for them to be experts in everything.

Fortunately, when stakes are low and the answer is not so crucial, leaders maintain or build trust simply by admitting when they do not know something and by setting out to find the answer.

The key to maintaining or to building credibility with others is to prioritize learning and development in order to maintain or achieve the level of competence required for your desired leadership role. Formal or informal education can do this for you so long as you strive to continually learn and develop. Even if you have a strong education it is important to be up to date on the latest developments because the world is ever changing.

Begin by identifying areas in which you should increase your competence and set goals to gain the necessary knowledge or skills. What issues do you need to know about? What will people expect you to know? Remember that you do not have to know everything to be an effective leader. Consider what you must know and what you can delegate. The following are a few ways to learn and develop as a Republican leader:

- Familiarize yourself with your organization's platform, bylaws or mission
- Know what is on the agenda in advance of a meeting
- Understand Parliamentary procedure
- Seek knowledge relevant to your organization

- Attend campaign management schools
- Participate in leadership trainings
- Follow current events
- Increase your involvement in your organization in order to achieve more organizational knowledge

Are there any means of development that you should prioritize for your current or desired leadership position?

EXPRESS HUMILITY

Working in a leadership position is usually regarded as an honor. This can create a certain amount of justified pride and self-esteem. Unfortunately, because a position of leadership in an organization hierarchy is above that of others, this can lead some leaders to believe that they are superior to others.

People are more likely to respect leaders who have a humble impression of their own importance. Leaders must understand that all contributors are important in an organization. Everyone in an organization has equal value. The organization needs both leaders and contributing team members to achieve results. One cannot exist without the other.

By acting in ways that show you value all of your team members, you will be trusted more and others will be more willing to give you the support you need for your Republican organization to be successful.

LEADERSHIP CHALLENGE

1) What actions can you take to maintain or build trust with people in your Republican organization?

2) Are you consistent in your words and actions? Are you who you say you are?

3) What information should you know to be effective in your leadership role? In what areas should you increase your competence? What issues do you need to understand?

4) How can you gain the information you need in order to be effective in your role?

5) In what ways do you express humility as a leader?

CHAPTER 2

Communication that Builds Trust

Trust may be the foundation of effective leadership, but communication is a key to building trust. People are more likely to trust people with whom they have a good relationship. Relationships are developed through communication. Learning communication techniques that build trust with and among Republicans in your organization is essential to your leadership development.

BUILD RELATIONSHIPS

Your ability to develop trust is influenced by the quality of your interpersonal relations. One reason for this is that people have a tendency to trust people they feel like they know personally. Others must be confident that they know you before they will trust you.

Thomas had a long successful career in the military and decided it was time to retire. He was also fed up with the direction Congress was taking the country. He decided to run for Congress in the town where he settled down with his family. However, he soon learned that he had a major obstacle to overcome. It did not take him long to discover that because he was a newcomer to the community, he was not trusted by party activists. In coffee shops around town people would say, "Who does he think he is?" or, "He can't represent us. He's not from around here."

This perception was a real barrier to the development of a strong campaign organization. His campaign team decided to work very hard to develop relationships with the townspeople. He began to go to local meetings and meet people in their homes. Trust began to develop as people learned more about Thomas and where he was coming from. In time, by engaging consistently, showing shared values and concerns for the community and by building personal relationships, Thomas built trust with the people. He was eventually elected to Congress.

For people to feel like they "know" you, they must know such things as how you think, what you believe and the values by which you live. You must be willing to take the risk of sharing information about yourself. Vulnerability is necessary. Some leaders do not reveal their identities because of fear of rejection and distrust. However, social distance actually causes distrust. For this reason it is important to increase your communication and interaction with others in a personal and informal way.

COMMUNICATE FREQUENTLY

Thomas also understood that to maintain the trust he had built with his constituents, he would need to continue communicating consistently with them after he was elected. This is because frequent communication builds trust. The following are some ways that Thomas was able to establish frequent communication with his constituents.

- Strong representation by his local office. His staffers engaged in the community as "eyes and ears on the ground"
- Town hall meetings when Thomas was in town
- Virtual town hall meetings by phone
- Online newsletters
- Online social networking
- Mailers

By communicating with constituents in all these ways, people felt as if they were in touch with their Congressman. They trusted Thomas and believed he was truly working for them. This same principle holds true for the grassroots leader. Effective leadership requires interaction with team members. Leaders who do not interact with their teams can lose trust and support. Consider the ways that you can maintain or increase communication within your organization. Do you need to increase communication with your team members in order to build trust?

Frequent communication also increases the quality of your decisions, because of the gained perspective you have from your connectedness. On the other hand, if you become isolated, you run the risk of making less effective decisions, due to possibly inaccurate or incomplete information. The following actions will help prevent isolation and the trust problems that can result from it.

- Interact with your team members in informal settings, such as social functions.
- Break down status barriers and develop relationships based on mutual trust and a genuine commitment to supporting the efforts of others.
- Avoid gathering too much of your information from a few trusted friends.

- Seek perspective from several types of sources (i.e. people, written and oral reports, casual conversations, attitude surveys, various news outlets, etc.)

INTENTIONALLY SHARE HELPFUL INFORMATION

Another key to building trust through communication is by sharing helpful information. How many times have you known leaders who withhold information from others because "information is power?" Some leaders share information only on a "need-to-know" basis. Unfortunately, "need-to-know" communication creates suspicion and undermines trust. It also reduces the information that others need to be effective in their work, which undermines the mission of an organization.

When permitted, freely share information that will help others. Do not withhold information to gain power over others. It is better for members of an organization to be as informed as possible. When you share helpful information with others, this indicates to them that you trust them with the information and it also causes them to trust you.

A Republican organization had both an elected board and a general membership. The board made decisions about numerous expenditures at closed meetings, and it never reported such information to the general membership. Even though none of the expenditures were imprudent, the very act of having numerous closed meetings caused suspicion and distrust. The general membership eventually responded by replacing the board members with representatives that promised transparency. How often have we heard people cry out for transparency in government? People value information. Even though there can be appropriate reasons to have closed meetings or sessions occasionally, it is wise to maintain a usual policy of open communication.

It can be particularly important to share helpful information during leadership transition. "Knowledge Management" is a term often used to describe strategic practices that help to build continuity in organizations. One simple example of "knowledge management" in many volunteer grassroots Republican organizations is simply the practice of passing on a notebook of some kind to the next leader. As simple as that may sound, if you capture "what you know" and pass on this perspective to the next leader, it will save him or her valuable time and they will not have to "reinvent the wheel."

Information sharing between transitioning leaders is an investment in the future of an organization and a springboard from which new leadership can launch its own unique term. By sharing information, others gain perspective, history and context. By sharing information you reduce redundant workload, reduce future training time for new leaders, and your teams adapt much faster to the changing political environment.

Consider all of the ways you can transfer information in your organization. The impact that you will have by introducing or maintaining these continuity strategies is efficiency and ultimately an advantage over the competition — the Democrats. The following are ideas for effective knowledge management in your organization:

- Educate others. Discuss with your organization the link between passing on knowledge and accomplishing your mission more effectively and efficiently.

- Keep records to pass on to future leaders.

- Encourage other leaders to keep records for future leaders.

- Build in an expectation of incoming leaders so that they maintain information for future leaders. Help them to understand that their term as a leader is not complete until they pass on resources to the next leader(s).

- Encourage incoming and outgoing leaders to meet in order to share insights, train, pass on resources, etc.

- Create your own techniques. Brainstorm with your team possible ways you can better your transitional processes.

Together, you will take pride in knowing you are leaving a lasting legacy in an organization you all believe in.

COMMUNICATE SPECIFICALLY

People look to leaders to provide goals and direction. When working toward a goal, team members are more confident when a leader is very specific about his or her expectations. When leaders are unclear, people become frustrated, feeling as though they are working blindly and without instruction.

A group of young Republican students were planning a campaign activist training for their members. Several students who were going to be trainers grew frustrated because they did not know what was expected of them. They knew they were expected to train, but did not know specifically what to do or how to prepare. Some of the members began to wonder if there would even be a training event.

Understanding that the students were busy and preferred e-mail communication instead of in-person meetings, the campaign activities chairman created a step-by-step preparation sheet for each student trainer, explaining what to do in order to be ready to present at the training. He e-mailed it to each student trainer. The students appreciated the specific details for how to prepare, and they better understood what was expected of them. Due to this specific communication, they felt more confident in the campaign activities chairman's leadership and they trusted more in the leader's ability to lead them to their final goal — a successful campaign activist training. Is there any communication for which you are responsible that could be more specific? How can you communicate more specifically with your teammates in order to help them to more effectively reach organizational goals?

BE KNOWN AS A PROBLEM SOLVER

Decision making is involved in all aspects of leadership. Making good decisions builds credibility. Leaders who are known as problem solvers are trusted and viewed as credible. After all, leading through challenges is the very essence of good leadership. If people are going to trust you to make decisions on their behalf, they need to trust your judgment. Great leaders are innovative and build teams of the most creative problem solvers they know, instead of pointing fingers and asking, "Who did this?" Great leaders ask, "What can we do? How can we fix this?"

Many times when a problem arises, leaders immediately blame others instead of problem solving. One problem with blame is that it is backward-looking. It leads people to look to the past instead of to the future. For this reason, blame is also inefficient, because if someone is busy trying to figure out "who" did it, they are not trying to solve the actual problem. When a person blames others all of the time, people begin to question his or her problem solving abilities.

EFFECTIVE DECISION MAKING PROCESS

Most of us are accustomed to thinking of a good decision as one that gets immediate good results. However, there are many decisions that are good, not because of results, but because of the process used to reach the decision. A good decision process enables a decision to stand up to scrutiny and even criticism that may follow. When you make a good decision, you should be able to look back on it, regardless of the visible results, and say, "I made the best possible decision at the time, given the information and other resources available."

The following six steps will help you to avoid the "blame game" and make good decisions:

STEP 1: Explore and Define the Problem

First, you must define the problem. That which appears to be the problem may actually be nothing more than a symptom of a more important problem. Also, sometimes we assume there is a single problem when there are actually two or more related problems. So, break it down. Take on one issue at a time.

STEP 2: Establish Decision Rules

Consider how, when, and by whom a decision will be made. By answering these questions, you can break a complex decision into manageable, smaller issues and assign responsibility and accountability accordingly. When time permits, include multiple people in the decision making process. This is helpful because other people can help to identify unforeseen issues. The added perspective will enhance the quality of your decision.

STEP 3: Consider Alternative Creative Solutions

Instead of accepting the first available solution, consider alternative solutions. During this phase, do not judge the ideas set forth. Instead, generate as many ideas as you can. A quantity of thoughts increases the quality of ideas and decisions.

STEP 4: Analyze Alternative Creative Solutions

Consider the solutions set forth and consider their worthiness. Consider advantages and disadvantages to each. This is the phase when you judge alternative solutions.

STEP 5: Choose a Solution and Take Action

Ultimately, a decision must be made. Sometimes we have more time to do this than at other times. The key is to make the best decision with as much information as you can possibly have at any given moment.

STEP 6: Implement Ideas, Seek Feedback and Adapt as Needed

Once a solution is chosen, take action. Once you see the results of your decision you will be able to analyze it and seek feedback from others. The ability to seek feedback, learn and adapt are critical to effective leadership. We often learn from the decisions we make. We grow as leaders by changing our future actions based on what we learned. Also, as time passes, changes in attitudes, values, technology, financial conditions or the introduction of new information may call for an adaptation of the original course of action.

How do you make decisions? Depending upon the complexity of the job, a more complicated decision making process may be required. The key is to understand that a good decision process enables a decision to stand up to scrutiny and even criticism when it is explained to others. A leader will maintain and build trust with others when people respect both how and why decisions were made.

LEADERSHIP CHALLENGE

1. How strong are your relationships with people in your Republican organization?

2. How can you increase communication in order to build relationships with and among your team members?

3. How can you establish consistent, frequent communication in order to build trust with and among your team members?

4. How do you gain needed perspective? Do you gather information from a few trusted friends or informants? How can you increase the accuracy and completeness of the information you receive?

5. Do you interact with others in your Republican organization in informal settings?

6. What possible status barriers might you need to break down in order to build relationships?

7. Do you intentionally share helpful information?

8. What information do you currently have in your possession or in mind that can help another member of your Republican organization do his or her job more effectively or efficiently?

9. In what ways can you or your organization increase open communication in order to build trust?

10. If you are going through leadership transition, what kind of information would be helpful to transfer to an incoming leader?

11. How can you communicate more specifically?

12. How do you normally respond when problems arise within your Republican organization? Do you find yourself looking for someone to blame? Or are you more focused on solving the problem?

13. Do you think people respect your decisions? Why?

14. How can you increase the quality of your decisions?

Motivating Yourself & Others

Do you ever wish you could motivate people in your political organization to become more active or to assume a more involved role? Do you feel like you have tried everything and that it is still difficult to motivate people, even during an election year? Since motivating others is at the heart of leadership, it is important to learn strategies in order to motivate yourself and others. As leaders, it is our job to discover what specifically motivates others. In this chapter, we will answer these questions:

- What factors indicate that a leader is motivated?
- How might others perceive your motivation level?
- How can you increase your own motivation level?
- How can you motivate other Republicans to become more active in the political process and in your organization(s)?

CHAPTER 3

Understanding Your Motivation Level

Who is the most motivated person that you know? What makes you think of this person? Likely, this person is someone who is positive, upbeat, busy and goal driven. This is also probably someone that you and others are inspired to follow because he or she is inspired and is taking action to prove it!

Tommy works in a State Representative's office and considers himself to be a highly ambitious young staffer with lofty political goals. However, Tommy also is an aspiring "Solitaire" champion. At any given time, you can find him playing the game on his office computer or phone. His colleagues find it annoying that he spends his "spare" time focused on this game. Because of the way others perceive how Tommy spends his time he would not be described as someone who is *motivated*.

On the other hand, Tommy's co-worker, Bonnie, follows up promptly with constituents each day. When she is finished, she looks for something else to do, helping other staff members with their work, running errands around the capital or brainstorming new strategies for getting information needed for bills that the representative is working on. Because of the actions Bonnie takes, her colleagues would describe her as highly motivated.

Motivating others is at the very core of leadership. In politics, we strive to motivate others to go to the polls "early and often", to vote a certain way, to volunteer, to give money, to spread the word, or to rally. If we are to increase our ability to motivate others to do these things, we must first be motivated ourselves. During an off-election year, it may seem difficult to keep Republicans fired up, but this is a must.

CONSIDERING YOUR OWN MOTIVATION LEVEL

People cannot help but make judgments about other people's motivation level, based on what they observe. Although the observation may be unconscious, leaders are often judged in this way. And if you cannot motivate other Republicans unless you are perceived as "motivated," then it is important for you to understand your own motivation level and how others might view you.

The key is for your actions to be aligned with what you intend to communicate as a leader. You may know that you are motivated, but what do your actions communicate to others? Here are some factors that will have a strong influence on the extent to which you are perceived as "motivated":

- Your perceived energy level (physical signals)
- Your hours of work (on a project, etc.)
- Your use of time (priorities)
- Your self-expectations and goals
- Your identification with organizational goals
- Your courage and drive to initiate

Your Perceived Energy Level (physical signals)

Are you tired? Does it show? Would people describe you as sleep deprived or energetic? What does your appearance or your behavior indicate about your energy level?

Your Hours of Work

Do others see you working? How much time do you spend contributing to the organization or project?

Your Use of Time

When others see you working, what do they see you working on? What kinds of projects do you prioritize? Are you willing to do whatever it takes to get a job done, no matter what kind of work it is? People will draw conclusions about what motivates you based on how you value various projects. How you use your time is a reflection of your values.

Your Self-Expectations and Goals

Do you have high expectations of yourself? Are you goal oriented? What do your aspirations or your lack of apparent goals indicate to others?

Your Identification with Organizational Goals

Do your decisions, actions and goals express your own interests or the best interests of the organization? Do you believe in the objectives of your organization and if so, how do your actions demonstrate this?

Your Courage and Drive to Initiate

Do you initiate new ideas and projects in your organization? A willingness to try new things and share ideas signals to others that you arc a go-getter, someone who forges ahead and takes action in order to reach organizational objectives.

Self-awareness about how you may be perceived is the first step toward increasing your own motivation level. If you identify your specific development needs, then you can consider specific ways to increase your motivation level. You are likely in an organization of very motivated activists, and would not be working in a Republican organization if you were not motivated yourself. However, if you need and want to increase your motivation level, it *can* be done.

LEADERSHIP CHALLENGE

1. How motivated are you on a scale from 1-10?
(1 = low; 10 = high)
    a. In your current role

    b. On a specific project

2. How motivated do you think others perceive you to be on a scale from 1-10? (1 = low; 10 = high) Is this different from #1? If so, why?
    a. In your current role

    b. On a specific project

3. How can this perception of you affect your present and future success?
    a. In your current role

    b. On a specific project

CHAPTER 4

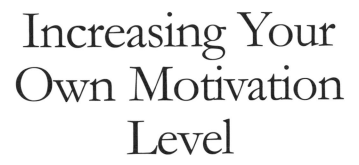

Increasing Your Own Motivation Level

It is critical that Republicans stay motivated. As a leader, you want to make sure that you are, too! People may think that they have no control over their own motivation level, but the truth is, if you prefer to be more motivated, you *can* increase your own motivation level.

Your thinking affects your actions and your actions affect your results. By understanding your motivation level and by acting in ways that over time will change your thinking, you can ultimately increase your motivation level. The following are just a few ways that may help you to increase your motivation level:

View Every Experience as an Opportunity to Learn What Motivates You

As you take on various positions or tasks in your organization, consider them opportunities to learn something about yourself. Some members enjoy managerial roles and other members prefer working on specific tasks. Some people are particularly motivated by specific political issues or causes. Figure out what fires you up!

Over the years, Ella served well in leadership roles that were highly conceptual, involving matters such as long-term goal setting and planning. Since she was very social, Ella worked best when she interacted with others. In contrast, she did not thrive in roles that required her to do bookkeeping, record keeping or data entry. So, when she was asked to be the club secretary, something inside told her she did not really want this position. Although she did not like the tasks involved, she accepted the job. Ella unfortunately did not learn from her previous roles what motivated her about the work itself. After taking the secretary position, she found herself to be highly unmotivated, and began to question her desire to remain a member of the club. She did not recognize that the problem was not necessarily the organization, but rather the role she was in. In time, she decided to quit the organization all together because she did not enjoy it the way she had in years past. When Ella left the club, her organization and the Republican Party lost a valuable, contributing member.

Every role we take can teach us something about ourselves. The better you know yourself and the more often you take on roles that fit your personality, work style, interests and preferences, the more motivated and effective you will be.

Take Responsibility for Understanding What Motivates You

Not only should we learn from our experiences, but we should also work proactively to figure out what motivates us. Consider the specific roles you have had in your organization or in other organizations. Ask yourself which ones you enjoyed and why.

- What are your gifts, skills and talents?
- How might you serve the organization utilizing these gifts?
- What are other people saying about you? What might they see that you do not see?
- What would your friends and teammates say are your strengths?
- Think of people who seem particularly motivated. How do they spend their time and what do they enjoy?

We all know that one of the characteristics of successful people is that they love what they do and do not perceive what they do to be "work." Figure out how you love to serve your organization or cause, and then focus on it and you will find your motivation level increases exponentially.

SEEK OUT AND/OR CREATE ROLES THAT YOU FIND MOTIVATING

If you have an interest in serving in a certain capacity, make an effort to ask about the position. Approach the person who is currently in the role to learn more about it. If there is a committee, ask if you can join it or observe meetings. Have you ever received a call from someone asking you to fill a position in the club? Did you want the job? If not, did you ask if there were other positions available or did you take it?

Tamara was asked to be the treasurer of a campaign for a county commissioner. She was so honored and excited to be asked to be a part of the campaign that she said "yes" without considering her work tendencies and preferences. After a few months in her new role, she found herself in a bind because the job was really made for someone who is both detail oriented and organized. Tamara had strengths, but attention to detail and organization were not two of them. Therefore, Tamara struggled with this role and regretted her choice as she fell behind in her duties and worried that others would begin to notice.

Rather than taking the first position offered to you, make sure the position is a good fit. You owe it to yourself to be honest about who you are and what kind of role would best suit you. You might be asked to take on a role that you really do not think is right. Ask follow-up questions about the job to confirm your belief, and do not be afraid to ask if there are other positions open that you could consider. If you have a particular talent or skill that would be helpful to the club and you would like to serve in this way, do not wait to be asked. No one may ever know to ask! Ask and you may find yourself in a new role because you spoke up.

Martha joined a Republican Women's Club. On the membership application that she filled out when she joined, Martha checked off "Membership Committee" and "Public Relations" as two committees that she was interested in joining. However, after six months, she realized that no one ever called her to notify her of a meeting or project opportunity. She began to notice that the person who was the Chairman of Membership did all membership tasks herself or alongside the president of the club. She also noticed that no one in the club was doing any publicity for the club. Instead of talking to someone about what she saw, she increasingly found herself uninterested in the club. Unfortunately for this club, a service organization in the same town asked Martha to head up Public Relations for their organization. She was thrilled and began to create a media contact list and media opportunities for that organization. Eventually she fell away completely from the Republican Women organization, where she did not feel she could make a difference.

Here is a valuable lesson to current leaders in organizations and to individuals interested in serving: both the organization and the individual member has a responsibility to communicate with the other about involvement. Organizations should not allow potentially great members to get away because they do not follow up. Failing to engage members can result in de-motivation, and ultimately a loss to the organization. On the other hand, if you are an individual who is interested in serving, who has communicated this interest but has not received feedback, try again. Take responsibility for increasing your motivation by ensuring your message is heard. Do not simply give up without having given the organization the opportunity to know you and capitalize on what motivates you, because once you find that role in the group, your motivation should increase greatly!

RESPOND PROACTIVELY TO NON-MOTIVATING CIRCUMSTANCES

When faced with a non-motivating situation, it is important that you address the issue and attempt to improve the situation. Otherwise, a prolonged period of de-motivation will negatively affect both your outlook and your output. If you find yourself in a misfit role, share your concern with another leader. You may ultimately determine that the role is not the problem.

Ted was asked to write the monthly newsletter for a local Republican county party. Ted was new to the organization and extremely excited to be involved. He expressed concern that this may not be the best task for him, but he was convinced by the county chairman that this was definitely a task he could do. The county chairman assured him that he would have ample help, and that the other county officers would send him information to include in the newsletter. After several months passed without anyone sending him any information, Ted was very disappointed. He was so new to the organization that he did not know enough about what to write. The county chairman did not intervene to help Ted productively write a newsletter either. This was terribly de-motivating to Ted, and he found himself regretting taking on this role, as it was not at all what he expected. Eventually, having experienced no success, Ted began to feel hopeless in the role.

Instead of giving up, Ted decided to become proactive about the newsletter. He began calling the various officers and committee chairmen in order to get information that he needed. He began asking everyone he could for perspective about the newsletter. He even found someone who gave him a newsletter template. By responding proactively to a negative situation and going after the resources he needed, he was able to reach his goal of constructing a newsletter. He was so excited upon its publication that he had a renewed sense of enthusiasm about his role. Instead of blaming anyone, he took personal responsibility for getting it done, and in turn he actually increased his own motivation level. Each month after that he was able to produce a newsletter and it became easier and easier each time.

It is a choice to do a good job in spite of occasional de-motivating circumstances. We have very few things we can control in life, but one thing we can control is how we respond to challenges. A great attitude can help us overcome just about any obstacle that comes our way.

LEADERSHIP CHALLENGE

1. Do you want to increase your motivation level?

2. What have your experiences taught you about what motivates you?

3. How can you learn more about what motivates you?

4. Do you deliberately seek out roles that are motivating to you? If not, what action can you take to find a role that is motivating?

5. If there is not currently a role that suits your special skills or interests in your organization, could a role be created for you? What steps should you take to find out?

6. Have you recently been faced with any kind of de-motivating circumstance in your organization? How did you respond? If it is still occurring, what positive action can you take that could possibly lead you to an increased level of motivation?

4. What behavioral changes, if any, should you make to increase your perceived motivation level in order to more effectively motivate others?

    a. In your current role

    b. On a specific project

CHAPTER 5

How to Motivate Other Republicans

In a contentious political climate there are likely very few Republicans who are unmotivated, particularly to vote. But even in these times it can be challenging for leaders to motivate people to do the very work that will help to get Republicans elected, such as phone calling, block walking, or social networking. Nevertheless, as a leader, you *must* motivate others. Motivating others is the very heart of leadership.

If you are the leader of a Republican organization, you probably have a goal to support and elect Republicans. However, there is no way that you can take on the burden of effectively accomplishing this goal by yourself. You need others to work with you. So how can you effectively motivate others to help achieve these goals?

There are two myths about motivation that are helpful for you to understand when considering how to motivate others: (1) There are people who are not motivated and (2) "Motivating" is something we do "to" other people.

Myth #1 about Motivation: There are People who are Not Motivated

"Bryan isn't motivated. He shows up at meetings, but he does not *do* anything." The speaker in this example assumed that Bryan is not motivated because of what he does not do. It sounds like there are other actions that the observer believes Bryan needs to take.

This assumption about Bryan is wrong, because everyone is motivated to do something — even if that something is nothing. If someone is slow to take action, he or she is probably just not motivated to do what you want him or her to do (or perhaps they are not even aware that you think they should be doing something). Your job as a leader is to learn what does motivate people.

In a board meeting, a group of Republican women brainstormed the names of women who could fill an open committee position. Vivian said, "I have a great idea! What about Nelda?!" Jennifer replied, "No. She won't work. We asked her to do that before and she said, 'No'."

What is wrong with Jennifer's response? When was Nelda asked about the position? Five minutes ago or five years ago? If it was five years ago, what was her reason? Is it possible that Nelda's circumstances have changed in five years? Maybe she was working two jobs at the time. Maybe she is now retired. Or possibly she was grieving the loss of a loved one and now she is ready to get out there and get busy.

When we make assumptions about the level of other people's motivation, we potentially lose opportunities. We will never know someone's true motivation unless we ask them personally about their current circumstances and interests.

Kelsey, a woman at the board meeting spoke up and replied to Jennifer, "Maybe we should learn more about Nelda's current circumstances. I know I am certainly capable of more now than I was two years ago when I became a mother. Seasons of life change. I hope someone would ask me what I want, and not assume that I'm incapable of contributing just because I turned down a position in the past." The ladies at the meeting agreed that they should contact Nelda to determine if she would be interested in and capable of serving at this time.

Leaders should consider someone's circumstances and also what interests them. What does each person do for a living? Or what did they do before retirement? What are their gifts and talents? The question to ask should not be, "Is that person motivated?", but rather, "What motivates that person?"

Evan, the president of a Republican young professionals organization, was looking for someone to fill a few vacant roles. He called Monica to ask her about one of the positions, and ended up offering her another. Why did he change his offer? When he asked about the first job, Monica declined, explaining how busy she was with another organization in town. However, during the conversation, Evan asked Monica what she did for a living. Monica told him that she used to be a librarian at a local school, but that she left this job to stay home with her children. Evan noticed that when she reflected on her work as a librarian, Monica's voice became enthusiastic. She stated that she had a real heart for literacy and missed her work. What Monica did not know, was that the organization was planning to create a new literacy committee. So, with his new-found knowledge about Monica's motivation level as it related to literacy, Evan shared with her his vision for an upcoming literacy project that would not only meet a great need in the community, but would also be a great service project for Republicans. In that moment, Evan found a new leader to oversee an upcoming book drive. Monica excitedly accepted the post of Literacy Chair, because she was personally motivated. She turned out to be a great leader, too. She took initiative, made a plan for the project, built a team and saw the project through to completion. Through this experience, Evan discovered the importance of learning about the members of his organization. He realized that in order to effectively match people to the right roles, he first had to learn what interested them. Only then would he be confident that a new leader would truly be motivated in a particular position.

If you are in a leadership role and learn of someone's special interest or skill, and he or she desires to use this skill to serve your organization, ask yourself if there is currently a complementing position available for him or her. If not, could a position be created for them? An active member is a motivated member!

MYTH #2 ABOUT MOTIVATION: "MOTIVATING" IS SOMETHING WE DO "TO" OTHERS

The second myth to consider when seeking to motivate others is the notion that "motivating" is something we do to others. As leaders, we sometimes take credit for motivating someone, as if we are a puppet master. We manipulate a few strings, and the other person responds the way we want them to. But, is "motivating" really something we can do to someone? No. Not really. "Motivation" is an internal state that directs individuals toward certain goals of their own. We cannot reach into the minds of others and compel them to do what we want them to. However, we can help shape and direct the motivation of others. The following are some ways that you can make an impact.

- Prioritize immediate involvement in your organization
- Discover people's specific needs, interests and talents
- Help people to identify with the organization
- Help people to see how their specific efforts connect to desired results — winning elections
- Remove as many barriers to member participation as possible

- Don't forget people who are already motivated
- Create group challenges

PRIORITIZE IMMEDIATE INVOLVEMENT IN YOUR ORGANIZATION

The President of a local Republican Club, Larry, realized that very few members of his organization were actually involved in club activities. Steadily, their group had grown smaller and smaller. After learning about the long-term benefits of an involved membership, Larry suggested that the club attempt to understand the interests of its members in order to bolster their activity level. The membership application form could ask about the interests of new members, while longstanding members could be provided a survey or even one-on-one phone call. He told his board that this was just the first step in membership development. The next phase would introduce members to the committees in which they were interested.

Larry asked the chairmen of various committees within the Republican Club to appoint members to their respective committees. However, noticing they did not respond, Larry decided to build the expectation into each Committee Chairman's job description. At the beginning of the new term, each committee would be comprised of a minimum number of members.

Larry sat with the board and went through membership forms that indicated committee preferences. They managed to assign each member to a committee. Larry then asked each Committee Chair to hold a kick-off goal-setting meeting for their committees. Chairmen were asked to report back to the board about the goals of their committee. Because of this initiative to prioritize the involvement of members in the work of the club, more members became active and felt a part of the organization.

Discover their Specific Needs, Interests and Talents

People are motivated to stay where they are welcome and needed. Therefore, it is imperative that your organization establishes frequent, consistent and multiple means of encouraging participation of new and established members. Larry did a great job of discovering his member's interests, through the survey process.

In an earlier example, Martha filled out a membership application for a Republican Women's Club. She was very excited about serving in the organization. However, no one ever called her regarding the interests that she checked on the form. In this instance, what did the Republican Women do well? They asked for the information up front when a new member joined the club. Asking new members about their preferences when they join is a great idea. But what about follow-up? The process is not complete without implementing a follow-up phase. Did the Republican Women have a mechanism in place to follow-up with new members in order to introduce them to projects and committees that might be of interest? This does not appear to have been the case, and unfortunately, losing a member was the result.

Therefore, remember to build follow-up into your membership development plan. After all, it is not unusual for some members to remain on membership lists without ever saying anything to anyone about their interests. Consider increasing the frequency in which you ask your members to join various committees or to serve in various roles. In fact, a great time to solicit interest is when projects arise.

Use multiple means of receiving this information, such as surveys, phone calls, or e-mail. Knowing what drives others will help you determine how best to match their interests with tasks to be completed based on broader strategic plans for election and organizational victory.

Help People to Identify with the Organization

Help new and experienced members see how their involvement is linked to a greater shared mission. In other words, make sure each person understands how their role is linked back to an objective of the organization. Keep your organization's mission in front of them. People are busier than ever and can join any number of niche clubs. So, it is imperative that they see the time spent with your organization as time well spent. What ways can you think of to help people identify with your organization?

Help People to See How their Specific Efforts Connect to Desired Results — Winning Elections

No matter what someone's role is in an organization, it is a valuable role. Even seemingly trivial or behind-the-scenes functions can be integral to the organization's success. Do not let a single person go without understanding how their tasks link back to the mission of the organization.

Ellen was woefully bored one afternoon because she had been stuffing envelopes for hours at the campaign headquarters for the local sheriff. Her mind would race. But mostly, she found herself wondering what the point of this job was. "Who reads these mailers anyway?" she thought. What she did not realize was the impact these mailers would make. The mailers would eventually serve purposes essential to a successful campaign, such as educating potential voters about the candidate's values and beliefs, and recruiting additional volunteers and campaign donors.

Had the Campaign Manager or volunteer leader on staff explained this to Ellen excitedly, perhaps she would have been more motivated, understanding the difference she was making. In fact, an even greater motivational experience might have occurred if the Campaign Manager had expressed how stuffing the envelopes would make the community a safer place to live because, "if elected, the Sheriff will…." Members in your organization enjoy and appreciate understanding the bigger picture and how they fit into the process. They feel valued, and are therefore more likely to be motivated and more productive.

REMOVE AS MANY BARRIERS TO MEMBER PARTICIPATION AS POSSIBLE

In many organizations there are barriers to member participation that have been identified or that go unidentified. Any barrier to participation means there is a barrier to member motivation, and therefore to action.

A young Republican professional's club was worried that they did not have enough young women in their organization. They identified that they had a number of women who were interested in going to the meetings, but who did not attend because they had small children at home. So, the club made a groundbreaking decision to begin budgeting money for childcare during their monthly meetings. Whose participation do you think they motivated? That's right, young mothers began to attend and volunteer because their barrier to meeting attendance was removed. Another women's organization was worried about low attendance of working women, so they began offering a night meeting alternative. Another organization began videotaping their daytime meeting and offering a night time potluck social where working members could attend and watch the program on video. Still another group changed their meeting time to the evening in order to motivate this target audience.

Another Republican Club struggled with a different challenge. Its members lived in a large rural district that made it very difficult for people to attend meetings. The drive was so long for members that they could not get back to work in time to make lunch meetings or would return home too late in the evenings after a long drive. The leadership team created an alternative "virtual" meeting to answer this challenge. This "virtual" meeting was a phone conference. Utilizing the phone, the members were allowed to conduct business and invite guest speakers from across the country (because speakers merely had to call in). Due to the success of the "virtual" meeting, the club grew in number and effectiveness.

- Identify potential barriers to your members' motivation.
- Prioritize these barriers from most crucial to least crucial.
- Brainstorm ways to remove the barriers.
- Take action to remove the barriers.

With these challenges identified and addressed, your organization can begin to thrive!

Don't Forget People Who are Already Motivated

It is important to keep those who are active and motivated, active and motivated. How do you do this? Reward positive behavior consistently. What are some ways that you can acknowledge people for a job well done? The following are several ways to help keep people motivated:

- Highlight the efforts of several members at meetings. This is free!
- Reward a member for a job well done at each meeting by giving creative "free" rewards. For example, allow someone to be the first person in line to eat and allow them to sit with the guest speaker.
- Identify a "Volunteer of the Month" or an "Employee of the Month."
- Create a special certificate that can be given to members any time they go above and beyond. You could call it the "Above & Beyond Award" and present them at meetings occasionally.
- Provide members with "Volunteer Highlights and Updates" or "Member Highlights and Updates." These can be announced at meetings and included in a newsletter.

- Allow business owners to share with the organization about their businesses, as an opportunity to promote their business among Republicans and to network.

Acknowledgement shows that you really see the efforts people make. It indicates that you value the actions of others and that you appreciate their efforts. It can be easy to take for granted our most devoted individuals and assume they will always be there. But, it is far wiser to find creative ways of praising them on behalf of the organization. These members are, after all, the heart and soul of the organization. What creative ideas do you have for motivating your most motivated?

CREATE GROUP CHALLENGES

Reaching a group goal can be fun and motivating to your organization. The following are ideas for group challenges:

- To generate a buzz about the upcoming election, an organization held a scavenger hunt. Members had to collect fifty items around the community. As members collected the items, they would explain what they were doing to the people they approached. In turn, many people learned about the election and the "Republican" viewpoint as well.

- As a twist on this idea, in order to motivate members to visit various campaign headquarters for the purpose of raising campaign work, the scavenger hunt could send members to various campaigns to pick up certain items or to attain the signatures of certain people after listening to a short presentation. In turn, members would learn where to volunteer, what types of needs the campaigns have, etc. Be creative in order to accomplish your goal!

- Another organization split their membership into two teams for a "Campaign Activities" contest. Each month, the members turned in their hours and added them up for their team. Upon a certain date, the team with the most campaign hours worked were treated to a potluck dinner by the other team! This activity was fun for members and it increased not only the number of hours volunteered in campaigns, but also the number of hours submitted to the record.

There are many methods to motivate teams and to generate excitement in ways that are linked to accomplishing your mission. First, identify what action you need members to take in order to reach a goal. Brainstorm fun techniques to reward members for achieving these goals. What creative ideas do you and your team have for generating excitement in your organization?

LEADERSHIP CHALLENGE

1. Do you want to motivate others to be more politically active or to serve on a particular project?

2. Are you aware of what personally motivates the people in your organization? (your team members, committee chairs, new members, etc.)

3. Is there anyone that you currently assume is unmotivated or disinterested in a project, but who may actually be interested?

4. Does your organization currently prioritize immediate involvement of its members? If so, how do you do this?

5. How can you and/or your organization ensure that you are learning the specific interests of your team members? (Surveys, membership applications, phone calls, club job fair, etc.)

a. Consistently

b. Frequently

6. What actions can your organization take to make sure that once you learn the specific interests of new or longstanding members that you use this information to help members find a role in the organization?

7. How can you help new and experienced members to see how their involvement in your organization is linked to a greater shared mission?

8. How can you help people to understand how their specific efforts connect to the intended result of your organizational mission?

9. Brainstorm with your team on possible barriers to member participation in your organization.

10. Prioritize any identified barriers to member motivation from most crucial to least crucial.

11. Brainstorm ways to remove each barrier to motivation.

12. Does your organization have a means of acknowledging the actions of your most prized members? In what ways do you thank and acknowledge these members publicly?

13. How can you generate organizational excitement and motivate your members to take action in ways that will help accomplish the organization's mission? What type of creative and positive group challenges might you be able to create? Make sure that the activity's mission is linked to an organizational objective.

* *

SECTION 3

Team Building for Republicans

Republicans must work together. Much is at stake in our country. Throughout the States, Republicans share a noble mission to limit the power of an ever-increasing and over-reaching government. You may be planning an event, working to elect a Republican candidate, drafting legislation or running for office — no matter what piece of the puzzle you work on, enhancing your team-building skills will help you to achieve your goal(s) more effectively and efficiently. In the following chapters, we will answer these questions:

- What are the four phases of team development?
- How can you help your team(s) to reach the "performing" phase efficiently?
- What are the characteristics of a high-performance team?
- What actions can you take that will improve your team's performance?

CHAPTER 6

Leading Republicans Through Phases of Team Development

Teams of Republicans are constantly forming and developing. At any given time, projects are starting or stopping. Dyck and Neubert, in *Management: Current Practices and New Directions*, indicate that there are four of these phases, including, "Forming," "Storming," "Norming" and "Performing." Republican leaders must be able to anticipate and identify these four phases and to lead Republicans through these phases in order to achieve the GOP's goals more effectively and efficiently. The four phases are as follows:

- Forming: A Team is Created

- Storming: Obstacles Emerge
- Norming: Habits Form
- Performing: A Team Excels

FORMING: A TEAM IS CREATED

A team forms when a new challenge is presented. For example: reducing a budget deficit, planning a fundraiser, a get-out-the-vote training or some kind of campaign activity. While energy is high, intentions are good and there is excitement during this initial stage, this may be tempered by team members' uncertainty about expectations, as the team does not know exactly how it will reach its goal.

A group of volunteers traveled from all over the state to have a block-walking day for a popular candidate, part of a larger "Get Out the Vote" effort. When they arrived at the campaign headquarters, they met people from all over the state, including the campaign team who organized the block-walking event. The campaign team welcomed everyone and began handing out the lists of addresses to visit in targeted neighborhoods. Excitedly, the groups of volunteers rushed out the door to their cars, ready for a fun day of block walking for their favorite candidate. After all, the election was the following Tuesday and this last push was going to provide the votes their candidate needed to win the election.

This team had begun the "Forming" phase of team development. This is an exciting stage that soon ends, particularly when a leader has not emerged to ensure that goals and expectations are clarified. To move a team beyond the "forming" phase efficiently, a leader should make sure that team members understand the goals and expectations as specifically as possible. If you are in this role, you should give team members as much information and as many resources as you can. Encourage communication among team members. Promote team organization and action planning.

STORMING: OBSTACLES EMERGE

Conflict is common during the "Storming" phase. Team members often feel discouragement and frustration. Team members question whether the goal is attainable. Team members often become concerned that conflict or other barriers will not be overcome. Some members may blame the leader or other team members for typical team problems.

Just moments after the group of volunteers arrived at their assigned neighborhood, Lilly, a veteran campaign volunteer began analyzing the list. "We need a plan," she said. As she reviewed the list of addresses, she realized that the addresses for the targeted Republican voting homes were not in a sequential order.

"This list is messed up," said Lilly, "In all of my years of block walking I have never seen a list like this. The addresses are not printed in order." She realized very quickly what the group needed to do. "Ordinarily, we could drive along, jump out and visit with residents at the homes along the way. Instead, I'm going to have to hunt for the addresses on the list that are on each street and then assign an address to someone to visit while out of the car," she said.

So at this time, Lilly emerged as the leader. However, along with identifying the problem and solution came a flood of opinions from other team members. Mike, who was also in the car, commented, "I don't think we're going to finish by 2 p.m. like everyone else." Kevin, who was looking at the list over Lilly's shoulder said, "Just give me an address. I'll go visit this house right here. It's on our list." Kevin grabbed some brochures, a door hanger and jumped out of the car. Others followed suit — after all, they could see houses that were on the list. So, they all jumped out and began working. Kelly followed Kevin, but discovered that the address she chose was way down the street. When she looked back she could barely see the car in the distance and felt very uneasy. "This isn't working!" she declared.

This team had entered the inevitable "Storming" phase of team development. In other words, the "honeymoon" or the

"Forming" phase was over. Now the real challenge that occurs with teamwork had begun. Why is this? Why do teams go through a "Storming" phase when they have the same goal?

Teams go through conflict because many perspectives exist. Everyone sees something different. Everyone also wants to reach the goal quickly and some members have different tolerance levels for how long it can take to find a "system" that works. People have different work styles, so someone who is a "doer" may grow impatient with the all-important planning phase and want to just "do" something. Sometimes this is necessary to get the group started, since some groups spend too much time trying to figure out what to do without taking action. When action is taken, it at least gives the team a starting place, from which to learn and make necessary adjustments. So, it makes sense that emerging perspectives and work styles would lead to frustration and an inefficient process.

How can you lead teams through the "Storming" phase? First and foremost, remember to remain calm and encouraging. If the leader becomes angry and loses poise, matters are sure to get worse. Instead, increase communication instead of avoiding it. Remind yourself and your team that this is a usual phase of team development. It will pass if you keep moving forward. Seek to identify and remove any barriers to your team's success. Consider whether members are in the right roles. Encourage members to move into the right roles, if need be, based on their strengths.

Lilly identified again for the team that they still needed a plan, a system. This had been a real barrier for the group already. She identified again that they really needed to let one person read the list, identify the addresses in order, assign the addresses and then let others visit those homes. One person would keep driving. Once everyone walking had a home assigned, the driver would drive to a location central to all or pick up walkers as they finished their assignments.

Although imperfect in the beginning, the group began doing this until they had a system. It was working! And the team got excited as they began to see how quickly they were knocking out one street after another.

NORMING: HABITS FORM

In this third phase, the team begins to feel optimism about its ability to be successful. Individuals begin to accept other team members and acknowledge their respective roles. Team members become concerned with specific deadlines.

The group settled into a pattern. Lilly would look ahead to find coming addresses on the street, put them in order and assign them to walkers. Then, the walkers would jump out and visit with residents at the homes along the way. The driver, Karen, would wait for the walker or drive to the end of the street and come back to pick everyone up in a central location.

When a team reaches the "Norming" phase, it would be understandable for a leader to think that their work is done. After all, the plan is now in effect and team members have found their groove. But is there more that a leader can do to lead teams to the finish line? Yes. Leaders should encourage the sharing of information and collaboration among team members. If it becomes apparent to the leader that there is any remaining confusion about the instructions they should clarify and reiterate expectations to keep the team from slipping back into the "Storming" phase. Ensure accountability. Keep the team's eye on the goal.

It was not long into the trip, when Karen realized she was maybe not the best person to be the driver. She was so focused on what the volunteers were doing at the doors that she nearly ran over one of her own volunteers. The group laughed, but Karen said, "Someone else needs to be the driver before I kill someone." One of the walkers mentioned that she had a bad knee and that it probably would be better suited for her to drive instead of walk. So the two gladly switched roles.

Lilly heard several of the team members make comments about things they had learned along the way. For example, Kevin pointed out that if people were not home, that they should still be leaving the door hangers, and warned another volunteer to be careful not to put brochures in the mailboxes, as this would be a Federal offense — mail tampering. Kelly pointed out that if there was a newspaper in the front yard, she would pick up the newspaper and take it to the front door as a nice gesture for the family.

When the team was back in the car driving to a new street, Lilly asked the team members to share their tips and concerns with one another. Kevin shared about leaving the door hangers and avoiding mail boxes. As it turned out, one of the volunteers was new at block walking and did not know this rule.

Thankfully, she had not placed any placards in mailboxes and was grateful to know the rule before she made a mistake. Kelly shared her practice of picking up newspapers and everyone liked this idea. Additionally, Lilly reminded the volunteers to please report the status of the household back to her when they returned, whether the volunteers spoke with someone or simply left materials. And also, she showed them how many homes they had already reached. The group was motivated to see that they were almost finished and this gave them the added momentum they needed to complete the neighborhood.

PERFORMING: THE TEAM EXCELS

In the fourth phase of team development, the team begins to have a sense of pride about their accomplishment. They gain confidence in their individual roles and as a group. They begin to consider the future and anticipate their next challenge.

Two hours into the block walking, the team of volunteers had their system down well. The walkers approached homes with a bounce in their step. Having visited numerous homes, they also had become comfortable talking with families. The speed at which the team was reaching each street had become faster. Everyone knew that Lilly was right and that this system was working. The team was cohesive and accepted the roles of their teammates. They began wondering if other teams of block walkers were finished already and how many homes other teams had reached. Instead of worrying about how they were going to accomplish their goal, the focus of their conversations had changed to the Tuesday election and the victory party they planned to attend. Eventually, they completed the entire neighborhood and let out a cheer as they finished.

This team reached their goal, despite the challenge they discovered with the tools they were given. They performed well. What happens at this point? Is the leader's work done? Not just yet! When the team excels and reaches its goal, a leader should provide feedback and rewards when possible!

Oftentimes, such as in this case, the volunteers are not motivated by money. So, praise, praise, praise! Thank team members for their service. Praises and a simple thank you are likely the most underutilized resources any leader has to give. If the project or program is recurring, the team should capture what it learned and record it for the next team who will take on this challenge. This way, when the process is repeated, the team can take into consideration lessons learned for better results.

Even though the campaign team was the leader at the beginning of the day, the real leader that emerged in this case was Lilly. On the way back to the campaign headquarters, Lilly reviewed with team members how many homes they reached. She was able to summarize their results and share with the group what she could see on the lists they were about to return. The team stopped by a fast-food restaurant and bought cold sodas as a reward, after a busy day out in the sun.

What do you think this team could have done in order to be even more successful? How could the Campaign Team leaders have made a difference? What could Lilly have done differently?

By understanding the phases of team development, you will be able to anticipate and manage the inevitable phases better. You will be able to move teams along more efficiently, particularly if you educate your team about these phases when the team forms, so that they, too, anticipate what is coming and are better suited to respond to it effectively.

LEADERSHIP CHALLENGE

(1) Are you in a leadership role currently? What team or teams do you lead?

(2) Which phase of development is the team in?

(3) Considering what you have learned what action steps you can take in order to help the team reach the next phase.

See the appendix for more information on the Phases of Team Development

CHAPTER 7

A Team "GPS" for Republicans

Leadership is an adventure. Every leader who has ever reached a goal has a sense of having conquered a mountain. However, while mountain climbing is challenging, there is very obvious equipment that a climber can use to help him or her reach the top. One such device is a compass. A compass provides direction. It helps us reach our goals. It can also help us to get back on track when we are not headed the right direction. These days, the compass is often replaced by a GPS unit. GPS can help us answer the questions: (1) Where am I? (2) What path can I take to get me back on the right path toward my desired destination?

Leading a team can be complicated. No matter your team-building skill level, it is inevitable that team challenges will arise. What if you had a TEAM GPS that could help tell you where your team is and help you get your team on the right path toward getting on track? When you are leading a team effort, use this navigation tool to think of ideas for team action. If a team is not performing effectively, review this list for action ideas. This is not an exhaustive list, but is a common list used to describe a high performance team.

- The goal or problem is clarified
- Communication increases
- The team gets organized
- Team members share ideas
- A plan is adopted
- Ideas are tried or implemented
- Team members understand their specific roles and responsibilities
- Some learning occurs through trial and error when trying something new
- Team learns from going through the process
- If first the team does not succeed, it tries again
- The team solves the problem or reaches the goal
- The team assesses its effectiveness and adjusts for better results
- Team members are moved into the right roles if need be, based on strengths
- The team repeats the process to create a system
- The team seeks feedback and assesses in order to continually progress

LEADERSHIP CHALLENGE

Consider a team that you are leading right now.

(1) Considering the actions taken by high-performing teams, is your team on track for success?

(2) Is the team experiencing any challenges? Are there barriers the team needs to overcome? If so, what are they?

(3) Upon review of the TEAM GPS are there any steps that have not been taken by a leader or by the team that could help you move forward toward your goal?

(4) Considering the possible team actions listed in the TEAM GPS, what steps can be taken in order to improve team performance?

* *

SECTION 4

Effective Delegation

Do you find it difficult to delegate when you know you should? If so, you are not alone. No matter how talented, experienced and capable someone is, delegating an important task may be difficult. To make matters worse, delegation is not simple. It is not simply giving someone something to do. Effective delegation is challenging, even for highly informed and experienced leaders. Nevertheless, effective delegation is essential. In this chapter, we will answer these questions:

- Why should you delegate?
- Why is it so hard for leaders to delegate?
- How do you know someone is ready for a task?
- How do you delegate effectively?
- How much should you delegate?

CHAPTER 8

Why Republicans Must Delegate

Do you do all of the work in your organization? Or do you and a few selected longstanding members of your organization do all of the work?

Elizabeth, the president of a local Republican Club found herself in this situation. She and the same small group of active members simply changed roles every few years, never adding any new faces to the leadership mix. Over time, the small group of people grew tired and one by one began to turn down positions for various reasons. When Elizabeth began to look for someone new to lead the organization, there was no one ready or willing.

This is because no projects were ever delegated to other members. Members outside of the group felt that they lacked the needed perspective to lead the organization or to feel confident taking on any kind of leadership role. Much like a basketball team with only five players, Elizabeth had no players on the "bench." Therefore, her lack of delegation over the years had created an organizational leadership crisis.

If Elizabeth's story sounds familiar, you and the Republican Party could be missing out on the numerous benefits that stem from exercising one of the most challenging leadership skills known to man — delegation. Delegation can feel very risky. Nevertheless, all Republican Party leaders must understand that effective delegation throughout our organizations will undoubtedly be a key to victory in elections.

Arguably, no leadership concept is more important than delegation. It is the process that empowers leaders to achieve organizational objectives by working through others. The concepts involved in delegation are deceptively simple. This is because while they are easy to understand, delegation is not always easy to do, even for highly informed and experienced leaders. When it comes to delegation, there is more than meets the eye.

BENEFITS OF DELEGATION

All leaders delegate to some degree, but some leaders delegate more than others. The following are benefits of delegating as much as possible, rather than as little as possible.

THE REPUBLICAN MULTIPLICATION FACTOR

Hector founded a very modest Hispanic Republican Club. He knew, however, that immediately he would need more members to help him achieve the organization's mission and perform certain tasks as elections approached. So, he recruited his first member. More and more people joined until Hector had a sizeable club.

At first, Hector did all of the work. As the organization grew, he found members whose strengths were different from his own. He could then delegate to members who were interested and capable of performing tasks that even Hector himself could not perform. Many organizations evolve like this one. They demonstrate the "multiplication factor" in delegation, the ability of a single leader to indefinitely assume increasing loads of responsibility by delegating.

Imagine the impact of the multiplication factor during an election year. If we delegate more to others in our organizations, there will be more active Republicans, which will translate into more Republican voters!

FREEDOM AND PERSPECTIVE

Delegation gives leaders the time needed to do work that is uniquely "leadership" work, such as planning and coordinating. If you do not have the time and freedom to think about the present and the future of your organization, you may not be delegating enough.

Alexis was the president of the High School Republicans. No matter what she did, she felt grossly overworked and constantly under pressure to get her work done. She expected so much from herself and rarely relied on others to help reach goals. She worked excessively long hours and skipped after-school events because of the demands of her position.

Linda, the next President, included many students to achieve their goals. Linda was a ground-breaking successful President. Because she utilized her delegation skills, it gave her spare time to help recruit new members.

The difference between the two leaders can be a matter of delegation. Effective delegation gives a leader the time needed to do work that is uniquely leadership work. Planning is the leadership function most often neglected by poor delegators. Unfortunately, poor planning leads to increasingly poor delegation, and the vicious cycle is reinforced. Leaders who are too close to their work fail to see the big picture. Only master delegators have the freedom and the perspective needed to actualize their full potential as leaders.

THE DEVELOPMENT OF NEW REPUBLICAN LEADERS

There are both new faces and longstanding members in our Republican organizations who do not feel as though they have a role in the Republican Party. One of the surest ways to give someone a voice is to give them a seat at the table. This inclusion is important for the present and future health of our organization. Every leader can find tasks that can be effectively delegated; this in turn, will free up the time needed to support these new members and leaders.

Effective delegation gives leaders the time needed to develop the skills and knowledge of other people. This is especially relevant since delegation is difficult, in some cases impossible, where the skill level of others is unknown.

Delegation itself develops others' ability to assume increased responsibility. People can learn to make certain types of decisions only if the leader is willing to give them the freedom to fail and learn from mistakes. Leaders who are afraid to delegate keep others from gaining the experience they need to develop. This limits the experience and perspective of others and therefore the organization suffers.

While managing a re-election campaign for a state representative, Max was elated when a group of volunteers from a government class at a nearby high school entered his campaign headquarters. However, after visiting with them, he realized that they had been assigned volunteer hours by their teacher as an exercise in political activism. The students did not seem motivated by their own interest in politics, but were assigned to be volunteers. Max picked up very quickly that they simply wanted to put in their time and leave.

The only work he had available at the time was phone-banking, which required communication skills. Unsure of how the students would behave on the phones, it is understandable that Max found delegating to the students to be a bit risky. But, Max reduced the risk by conducting a short training and practicing relatively close supervision until it was obvious that the students were capable of assuming the responsibility and they understood the importance of the task.

High Motivation and Morale

Effective delegation tends to produce high motivation and morale. Poor delegation has just the opposite effect. Morale is the collective positive or negative attitude of a group toward their organization. When more members of an organization assume a high level of responsibility, morale improves. We need as many champions for the Republican Party as we can get. After all, active members are more motivated to vote, donate their time and also give their much needed money to the Republican Party.

A Republican Pachyderm Club leader named Natalie seldom delegated. She did not build teams within the organization or give committee chairmen the freedom to develop teams. Instead she managed every committee job herself. She wondered why other members seemed critical of her and unconcerned about achieving her objectives. What she could not see was the effect that her lack of delegation had on other leaders in her organization. They felt as though they did not matter to Natalie.

People who are given responsibility and the freedom to make decisions on their own tend to feel more a part of an organization. A degree of self-esteem usually results from the assumption of responsibility. Natalie's failure to delegate to other members in her club resulted in membership alienation and hostility.

Reasons Republicans Do Not Delegate

If the benefits of delegation are so great, why is it so difficult to delegate? Republicans struggle with delegation for the same reason that Democrats do. This is a non-partisan issue. Leaders fail to delegate for a variety of reasons. Just being aware of some of the causes of poor delegation is of some help in avoiding these traps. If you identify with one or more of the reasons listed below, you are not alone. These are common causes of a lack of delegation:

Lack of Knowledge and Understanding

Lack of knowledge and understanding about how to delegate is most likely to be a cause of poor delegation for a person who is new in a leadership position. However, the "how to" of delegation is easy to learn. Kudos to you for reading this chapter to gain knowledge about how to delegate effectively! Already you have increased your odds of becoming a better delegator.

Low Value Placed on Delegation

Many leaders are not aware of how much they stand to gain by delegating well and how much they are losing by delegating poorly. Failure to value delegation is widespread. Do you value delegation? What action do you take that shows others you value delegation highly?

Insecurity and Risk Avoidance

Considerable risk is involved in delegating, especially when leaders are not close enough to others to know their strengths and talents. However, because of a fear of failure and a lack of control, many leaders still find it challenging to delegate, even when they know others' strengths.

Low Awareness of Others' Abilities and Motivation

To be an effective delegator you must know the capabilities of others on your team or in your organization. Because of this, leaders who relate to others informally and enjoy open two-way communication have major advantages over those who are isolated.

Avoiding the Appearance of Laziness

New leaders sometimes feel that when they are performing leadership functions, such as planning and coordinating, that they may not be seen as "working." They feel they should be producing something tangible or helping with the physical and mental tasks in which other people are engaged.

Consider Alice, a long-time Republican Party county treasurer who was recently elected to Chairman of a county party. Even though her role changed completely, she continued to do routine accounting work for the party, even though there was someone else with the title of "treasurer." Alice felt that she had to be doing a task to feel productive. Compared to the financial reports that she was accustomed to presenting, managing and facilitating did not feel like an accomplishment. Eventually, a close friend pointed out to Alice that she seemed to be too involved in the details of the treasurer's work and as a result was failing to perform critical functions of her actual job. The friend encouraged Alice that by delegating to others, building bridges, creating new projects, and problem-solving, she would be more productive.

Fear of Losing a Prized Role

In some situations leaders try to make others believe that they are the only ones capable of performing certain tasks. This makes them feel important and needed, but to people who see the situation for what it is, this communicates quite the opposite. It is often obvious when a leader avoids selecting strong individuals as team members. And if they accidentally select a strong team member, they do not always give them an opportunity to show what they can do. Soon, the strong and competent either leave the organization or become so alienated that they seek anonymity. In such situations, others are usually aware of what is going on, except for the fearful leader.

Unrealistic Feelings of Superiority

With the title of "leader" can come honor and pride. Suddenly, people want to know what you think about various issues. You may be invited to more events. You may be making more decisions than ever. This can sometimes give leaders an inflated opinion of their own importance and competence. An inflated sense of importance can lead to thinking, "I'm the only person that can do this right," which results in a lack of delegation.

The "I Can Do it Better and Faster" Myth

It may be true that you can do a job better and faster than someone else. But if you subscribe to this kind of thinking, it will likely always be true. If you never take time to invest in others, no one but you will ever know what to do.

Teaching someone else may take more time in the beginning, but ultimately it will save time. Every task that you believe you cannot delegate limits your potential for assuming additional responsibility. It is easy to fall into this trap. Are you delegating? Have you invested time in someone to help him or her start on a task that you should delegate?

Preference for Non-Leadership Work

If you are in a leadership role, you have likely heard someone say, "I'll do anything. Just don't make me the leader. Just give me something to do and I'll do it." The reality is, every organization has task masters. There are many people who have the preference of working on specific tasks instead of working in a leadership role. Any one of us may have an interest in avoiding leadership roles from time to time, depending on our season of life.

A problem can arise when a person is in a leadership role and they prefer non-leadership work. Some leaders simply love doing the kind of work they did before becoming a leader. This can create a situation in which a leader inadvertently works on details in the organization that should be delegated. If you identify with this, challenge yourself to consider whether the tasks you are working on could be delegated.

Excessive Desire to Please

You can't please everyone. You have to make tough decisions sometimes. An excessive desire to please can create a challenge for leaders. Leaders who have a strong need to belong are especially likely to withdraw into the safety of non-leader duties that should be delegated, while neglecting leadership duties that may produce conflict.

Perfectionism

A few leaders are such perfectionists that they panic at the thought of something going wrong. Unfortunately, when leaders delegate rather than do the work themselves, they fear that the likelihood of something going wrong increases. To reduce mistakes, they take on heavy workloads for themselves, including involvement in minor decisions that they should have delegated to others. And the results of others' work seldom measures up to the perfectionist's expectations.

If you are someone who is a perfectionist and you have trouble delegating, just remember that if you let go and delegate to someone else, things may not always be done exactly how you would have done it; nevertheless, the job *will* get done. You will find that giving someone else the opportunity to lead can be rewarding in itself and ultimately you will be more productive.

LEADERSHIP CHALLENGE

1. Do you believe that you should delegate more? Why?

2. What benefits will you gain if you delegate more?

3. What benefits will your organization gain if you delegate more?

4. Do you personally find it difficult to delegate? If so, why?

CHAPTER 9

Effective Delegation Skill Building

Delegation can feel like risky business to many leaders. The good news is that when you delegate effectively you actually reduce much of the risk involved. This is because effective delegation requires increasing the amount of communication between the delegator and the delegatee, which brings about more of a meeting of the minds. A better understanding about the expectations of the delegator eliminates the fears of both parties.

REDUCING RISK IN DELEGATING

One of the most challenging aspects of delegating can be the uncertainty of knowing if someone is ready to be assigned a particular task. If you do not know if someone is truly ready for a task then you are likely to have fear of delegating to them. There is a technique that you can use to determine how ready someone is for a task, but it requires you to know the person or to learn more about a person. (1) Identify the task that you want to delegate and consider what it will involve; (2) Analyze the prospective person's ability to complete this task; and (3) think about this person's commitment level.

Sometimes a person's commitment level is higher than their capability, but if given a chance and some support, this person can become the best kind of team member. Studies show that the more a leader delegates to someone, the more capable that person becomes. He or she can handle even more responsibility because they have added experience and perspective. Also, the more responsibility one has in an organization, the more committed he or she becomes.

Kristie was a very successful bank executive who had been in a Republican Business Club for two years. When she was asked if she would take on the role of Programs Chair for her club, she did not believe that she was ready for the task. Knowing what was required of the job and knowing Kristie's abilities, the president of the club knew that Kristie was more than capable of being successful in this role, with guidance and support. However, Kristie could not be convinced of this by the club president. The president realized that because Kristie had no prior experience working on a committee or on a project in the organization, Kristie felt as though she did not have enough understanding of the organization to be effective in this role.

Had she been responsible for a smaller task in the past, she might have felt prepared. Sometimes it comes down to confidence. If a person does not feel ready, no amount of persuading will convince them. Delegation itself develops people's ability to assume more responsibility. This club president learned that if you do not delegate small tasks to new people, they will never feel ready to lead.

Five Steps of Effective Delegation

Very often when leaders believe that they have delegated a task to someone successfully, and then the person does not follow through with the task, they blame the person to whom they delegated. However, the reality is that sometimes the leader contributes to the problem without realizing it. Instead of blaming, it is helpful to consider how you contributed to the situation. By taking these five steps, you can reduce the amount of risk involved in delegating and feel confident that you have delegated well:

STEP #1

Select someone whose talent matches the task (and who has the time and inclination to serve on a particular committee or to complete a specific task). This is a critical step in the delegation process. A leader cannot reasonably hold someone responsible unless that someone has the ability to perform.

STEP #2

Clearly assign the task to be achieved. Specifically communicate what is to be done. Sometimes we are so familiar with what a job requires we take for granted the details that are involved. So, we are unintentionally vague, and assume they have the knowledge to fill in the gaps we have left out.

STEP #3

Provide necessary resources. Resources that someone may need to complete a task could be access to certain people and information, the right to control specified budgets, facilities, equipment, and technologies, or authority over a committee, etc. Be sure to share the resources that you are aware they need. Then, it is good practice to ask them if from their perspective there is anything that they need that you have not provided. Very often needs are discovered after the person begins the task. Assure them that you are aware of this and that you have an open door policy, should they need to come back to you for something.

STEP #4

Make sure the person actually signals to you that they assume responsibility. You can ask the person to review with you what you discussed. One way of accomplishing this would be to ask, "Are you comfortable in doing this task? Share with me your understanding of what you will do, so that we can make sure we are on the same page." This can help to clarify any questions or concerns the person may have about the assignment.

STEP #5

Respectfully hold the person accountable for results through encouragement, goals and deadlines. A leader should follow up to ensure that delegated tasks are completed as assigned. This way, the leader can provide needed support or adapt the assignment if the situation warrants. The key is to keep in touch while avoiding supervising so closely. One means of doing this is to agree with the person on a date that you will follow up in advance of the final deadline. This way the person expects that you will follow up. This is helpful not only for people who need the added accountability, but also for people who are high performing, but particularly sensitive to close supervision, perceiving any call to be micro-management. When you call them, they will not be caught off guard and defensive because you followed up.

Without these five steps effective delegation has not occurred. If delegation was merely giving others something to do, every leader could easily become an expert delegator, and leaders with superior delegation skills would not be so rare.

HOW MUCH SHOULD YOU DELEGATE?

If you want to achieve only small objectives, you may be able to perform all the required tasks yourself. If you want to achieve moderately ambitious objectives, first delegate those tasks in which your skills are limited or, perhaps those you dislike performing.

If you truly want to make a lasting impact on the people around you, grow your organization and the Republican Party, all while increasing productivity in activities that help elect Republicans, you should delegate as much as possible instead of as little as possible. Delegating is one of the noblest actions a leader can take, because it is an action that is often behind the scenes and unnoticed by others, but is action that is taken in the best interest of the organization.

LEADERSHIP CHALLENGE

1. How can you personally reduce risk in delegating?

2. This chapter identified five steps in the delegation process. Which of these steps is challenging for you?

3. What goal(s) can you set in order to become a better delegator?

See the appendix for a Delegation Checklist and a Delegation Checklist for when someone delegates a task to you.

SECTION 5

Communication

Communication is an essential leadership skill. Leaders are often judged by how well they communicate. After all, every aspect of leadership requires you to communicate with others. However, some leaders find that they have a tendency to be non-assertive, or to the opposite extreme, overly assertive and these extremes limit their potential. By finding balance in their communication style, leaders can greatly enhance their ability to build influence. In the following chapters, we will answer these questions:

- How are your communication skills linked to your ability to lead others?
- Do you need to develop your communication skills?
- How can you communicate to others that you are listening?
- What is your predominant communication style?
- Do you need to adjust your level of assertiveness in order to maintain or increase your leadership effectiveness?

CHAPTER 10

★ ★ ★

Introduction to Communication

Communication is most simply defined as the process by which messages are sent and received. These messages may be expressed in many different forms-in letters, e-mails, texts, social networking, face-to-face conversations and even nonverbal clues by our body language.

Communication skills greatly contribute to or detract from a leader's success. Leaders are often judged by the way they communicate — their fluency, vocabulary, spelling, grammar and diction, along with other aspects of communication such as what their actions communicate.

According to Dyck & Neubert in *Management, Current Practices & New Directions*, communication involves four steps: forming a message, selecting a communication medium, sending a message and receiving a message. The key to good communication is to increase the effectiveness with which your intended messages are sent and received.

PHASE #1 — FORMING A MESSAGE

In the first phase of communication the intended message is translated from an idea into such symbols as words, gestures, facial expressions, and actions that represent the message that you mean to send. The development of your ideas may occur immediately or may be formulated over a period of hours or days. Sometimes you have a lot of time to consider what and how you should communicate; other times you do not. The more important the message, the more critical it is for you to develop your idea.

PHASE #2 — SELECTING A COMMUNICATION MEDIUM

The second phase of the communication process is when you choose the communication medium, or the method through which you send a message to the receiver. There are many ways to send a message. So you will want to choose the appropriate method of communication for the type of message you intend to send.

As you read the partial list below and if you use that method of communication, ask yourself whether you use it as effectively as you can:

- Face-to-face
- Telephone/Voice Mail
- Phone Conferencing
- Video Conferencing
- Business or Personal Letters
- E-Mails
- Internet-Based Postings
- Social Networking

- Newsletters
- Posters and Signs
- Billboards

There is no substitute for one-on-one, face-to-face communication when it comes to sending a clear message. This is because, when you are with someone in person, you can fully communicate through your words, body language and tone of voice. The type of communication medium that you choose affects how people interpret the meaning of your message. For example, when you send an e-mail you lose both body language and tone of voice, often leaving much interpretation of the message to the reader's imagination.

You must consider the nature of the communication. Is the message ready to send? Do you have all of the information you need? Is the message important? Is it formal or informal? Should it be discussed privately? While we love e-mail for bringing the world together and for saving us time, we also recognize how easily it can be misused. Because it is so easy to send a quick message to someone anywhere in the world, it is easy to hit "Send" without much thought as to whether e-mail is the proper method of communication.

Bill was the Chairman of a Republican law student association. One day while he was at school, he found out from a classmate that Ava, the Chairman of Public Relations of this association, was overheard endorsing John Doe, a candidate in a Republican Primary, to the media. Their organization had a strict policy that prohibited all officers from endorsing candidates during the primaries, in order to maintain the appearance of fairness. Bill was very angry when he heard this news. He wanted to talk with Ava right away.

However, he did not have time to find her or to call her because class was about to start. So what did Bill do to save time? He decided to send Ava an e-mail. He searched through his e-mail and found the last e-mail that she had sent, which included the club newsletter, and he hit "Reply." Bill then proceeded to type his thoughts to Ava in the following e-mail and then hit "Send":

"I can't believe you endorsed John Doe to the media. That was a dumb thing to do. You know this is against our rules. And besides, why in the world would you vote for John Doe? You can't be serious! Now, I'm going to have to clean this up, and YOU are the Chairman of Public Relations. Well, at least you used to be...."

The choice that Bill made has become a classic mistake. It is amazing how much damage a person can do with just the click of the word "Send". As an exercise, how many problems with Bill's actions can you count?

The first problem is that he chose to e-mail Ava about important organizational business that was better suited for a private discussion. Bill could have asked questions and learned more information. Instead, he acted on partial information and never found out whether the accusation was true. As it turns out, the person who told Bill about Ava's endorsement was mistaken about what she overheard. Ava was never given the opportunity to explain what really happened — until it was too late.

Bill was horrified when he realized that his e-mail was sent to the entire membership accidentally. Since Bill did not begin a new e-mail, everyone in the club received Bill's impulsive message to Ava. What will be the likely consequences of Bill's mistake?

- Due to his position, there are likely people who had a lot of respect for Bill, who will reconsider their perspective about him due to this e-mail. Bill will likely lose some influence with others.

- Ava may also lose influence with others who never hear her side of the story.

- Because the e-mail was sent to the entire membership, this was the equivalent of reprimanding someone in public, which is usually unadvisable. It is better to praise in public.

- Bill gave others a glimpse into his character because of the demeaning words he chose to write to Ava.

- Bill shed light on his own political stance in a Republican primary race, which is against his organization's policy. Immediately upon this news arriving at John Doe's campaign headquarters, Bill will likely lose the trust of the candidate and his followers. Doors once open to his association will likely shut.

- The association may lose Ava, a valuable member of his organization, because of Bill's actions.

- Other members of the organization may quit the organization due to his actions, out of support for Ava or for their preferred candidate, John Doe.

- Bill may lose his job as the president of the Republican Law Association.

- This type of mistake will follow Bill. E-mail is forever.

The list of consequences for Bill's mistakes is endless. Perhaps you can think of others. The cost of Bill's actions and his ability to lead effectively stems as much from his choice to send his message in an e-mail as it does with the content of the e-mail itself. What method of communication do you think Bill should have chosen? How could choosing a different method of communication have saved Bill as a leader and Ava's reputation?

In order to choose the appropriate method of communication through which to send a message, you must first determine who is to receive the message. Once you know who is supposed to receive the message, consider how he or she best receives information.

For example, does the receiver prefer phone calls or e-mail? Does he or she always respond to texts but never picks up the phone? Can you always find him or her on a social networking site? It is necessary for you to know the perspective and preferences of your team members — and for him or her to also know how best to communicate with you. Consider the following messages and what method(s) of communication should be used for each:

You are the president of a local Republican organization and are planning a debate for a statewide race during a Republican Primary. You want people to know that your organization is hosting a debate, and you want as many people to come as possible. The event is open to the public.

Intended Message: Come to the debate.
Intended Receiver: Public

- Face-to-Face conversation
- E-mail
- Social Networking site
- Public announcements through various types of media
- Phone call
- Personal written invitation

Every type of communication would work in this example. The key here would be to find out what works best for your area. Some organizations take ads out in local newspapers. However, in certain areas these types of ads do not work at all. Nonetheless, public announcements reach out to many people. Developing relationships with TV, Radio and newspapers will increase your organization's chances of receiving coverage.

Lola is a member of your organization. You would like to know if she can serve as a greeter at the debate.

Intended Message: We would like you to serve as a greeter.
Intended Receiver: Lola

- Face-to-Face conversation
- E-mail
- Social Networking site
- Public announcements through various types of media
- Phone call
- Personal written invitation

As mentioned in this chapter, face-to-face is often the clearest way to send a message, next would be a phone call. If you know Lola well, then you should know how best to contact her with this type of question. Oftentimes, the more personal your request, the better response you will get. It is harder to say "no" to someone in person, while looking them in the eye, than it is in an impersonal e-mail.

There are four candidates that you would like to invite to participate in the debate.

**Intended Message: We would like to have you participate in the debate.
Intended Receiver: Four Candidates**

- Face-to-Face conversation
- E-mail
- Social Networking site
- Public announcements through various types of media
- Phone call
- Personal written invitation

Depending on the type of race that this is, for example, if it is a state senate or house representative race, then sending an e-mail invitation to the scheduler will usually work, instead of to the candidates. Of course if you know a candidate or see a candidate, it does not hurt to mention it, but the candidate is not always the one who makes the schedule. It is best to follow up with the scheduler.

The more formal the event or the higher the office the more formal the invitation should be. If it is a local race, contacting the candidate directly may work if he or she does not have a scheduler. The key is to always know your specific receiver. Ask him or her how is the best way to communicate with them. Each candidate may need to be handled differently.

You need to visit with the committee working on the debate and want to weigh the pros and cons of asking particular questions during the debate.

Intended Message: We would like your opinion about whether or not we should ask this question.
Intended Receiver: Small Group of Debate Planners

- Face-to-Face conversation
- E-mail
- Social Networking site
- Public announcements through various types of media
- Phone call
- Personal written invitation

The first and last meeting should probably be face-to-face. This is a very sensitive topic which needs special attention; therefore, much attention should be given to the message formation phase of the communication to take place in the debate. Watching a person's body language is extremely important. Other people on the committee might say that they agree with you about a particular question, but their body may communicate something else, of which you should be aware. Conference calls could be used, but you would lose valuable clues found in body language.

PHASE #3 — SENDING

The third phase of communication is the actual sending of the message. This is when you actually talk with someone on the phone or hit "send" on an e-mail. Sometimes, the messages we send are not at all what we intend. For example, a person may interpret a short and direct e-mail as rude or angry when it was not intended that way. The interpretation is often more about the receiver's perception than the sender's.

PHASE #4 — RECEIVING

This brings us to the fourth phase of communication, in which the message is received. The receiver interprets the words, gestures or body language used by the sender. The message is given meaning, based on the receiver's perspective. A person's perspective or point-of-view is based on their backgrounds, education and experience.

To the extent that the sender and receiver have common perceptions and give the same meanings to the information, the sender is able to communicate successfully.

BARRIERS TO COMMUNICATION

If a message was not received the way it was intended, clear communication did not occur. For example, you can shake your head "no" while saying, "yes." Is this a clear message? People often communicate less clearly than they realize. Various types of barriers stand in the way. It is imperative that Republicans identify barriers to communication in order to increase their ability to get their message across.

Lack of Assertiveness and Self-Confidence

Often, especially in meetings, the people who are the most assertive and confident express their ideas. Sometimes the best ideas remain in the minds of people who do not speak up. This is because shyness, a lack of assertiveness or a lack of self-confidence can be a barrier to communication for some individuals.

Defensiveness and Threat

Defensiveness consistently distorts communication. If a leader is defensive when others come to him or her with ideas or concerns, then people will become cautious about the information with which they approach the leader. By reducing threat and building trust people will be more likely to communicate with you.

Gatekeeping

Gatekeeping is the process through which a member of an organization obstructs the free flow of information. A gatekeeper decides which information will be held back and which will be passed along in the communication chain on a "need to know" basis. Gatekeeping can take place at all levels of an organization.

A Climate of Distrust

Where conflict has long existed between people or between leaders, the chief barrier to communication may be distrust.
See the Trust Building chapter for more information.

Status Barriers

There can be the perception that someone in a political office or in an office of leadership is of a different status than other people. Keep in mind that this type of thinking can become a barrier to communication with such leaders. People who perceive themselves to be at a lower level of leadership sometimes do not feel comfortable communicating openly and freely with persons higher up in an organization. As a leader, it is important to be aware of this possibility and to do everything you can to break down perceived status barriers. By doing this you will keep lines of communication open.

Not Listening

There are many types of barriers to communication. One of the most common barriers to communication is the inability to listen. Most of us spend considerable time in our lives learning to speak and write; however, we spend little or no time learning how to listen. Yet, listening is one of our most critical communication skills.

As a Republican leader, it is imperative that the people with whom you work know you are listening to them. Your team members must believe that their voice matters or they will not be productive members of the organization. Individuals who do not feel heard usually feel defensive and suspicious. And, when someone's point of view is perceived to be ignored, emotions can eventually escalate. On the other hand, when people feel as though their perspective has been heard, they are more likely to participate and cooperate. This is because they feel valued.

When you work with people regularly in organizations, it is often not about one moment or one conversation, but what your actions communicate over time. Certain actions over time can make people feel like their perspective is important to you or to your organization or they can communicate that you or the organization is not listening. The following are ideas that will help you or your organization to send a message that you are listening:

#1 — Listen to each party's perspective before expressing your own.

It is human nature that when our perspective is recognized by others we become more attentive, sympathetic, understanding and appreciative of other people's ideas and perspectives. Negotiation and conflict research continues to indicate that when people feel heard, they are more likely to listen.

#2 — Exhibit traditional signs of active listening when in discussions

Active listening involves sending a message, through your words or body language, that you are listening to what is being said. Below are examples of ways you can demonstrate active listening:

- Do not interrupt
- Make eye contact
- Lean slightly toward the person
- Nod your head to let them know you understand
- Concentrate on what is being said
- Clarify by asking questions
- Rewind and repeat what the speaker says

#3 — Ensure a proper environment for listening

People are more open to providing information in a neutral trusted environment or at their own meeting. Visit auxiliary organizations to listen with an open mind, not as a spy or judge. Some leaders assign official liaisons to auxiliary organizations in order to multiply their efforts and to show their support. Questions to consider are, "What do we have in common? How do they need us? How do we need them?"

#4 — Beware of the tendency to compete

Occasionally check your motives to make sure you are not competing with Republican organizations or other Republicans unnecessarily. If there is a perception that you are competing with someone else, he or she will be unlikely to hear what you have to say.

If there is another Republican organization that your organization competes with, it is unlikely that you listen to each other's concerns or interests. If you do not listen to one another, you will not take to heart each other's endeavors and support one another.

#5 — Build trust and collaborate

Authentically build trust in all ways that you can. If someone does not trust you or your organization, he or she is not likely to listen to what you or your organization has to say. Set up a meeting with leaders of other organizations with the intention to build trust, learn more about their organization and to explore ways you may collaborate to achieve a common goal or mission.

See the Trust Building section of this book for more information.

#6 — Seek feedback

One way to show people in your organization that you are listening is to ask them questions. Seek their input so that they are included in decision-making processes. This will send the message that you respect and value the perspective of all people in your organization.

Brainstorm all of the current communication mediums that are available to your organization. Explore ways that you and other people in your organization can use them to receive feedback (i.e. direct communication, surveys at meetings, online questionnaires, phone conferences, forums, etc.).

#7 — Take action based on feedback received

When people provide feedback time and time again and never see any action taken based on this feedback, they begin to believe that their voice does not matter. One of the best ways to show others that you are listening is to take action based on what you learned from them.

LEADERSHIP CHALLENGE

1. Do you utilize various methods of communication effectively?

2. What is your preferred method of communication?

3. What are the preferred methods of communication of each of your team members?

4. In your current role, do any barriers to communication exist between you and another person or between your organization and another organization?

5. If needed, what steps can you take to improve communication?

6. In your conversations, do you usually exhibit active listening?

7. How can you ensure a proper environment for listening during your meetings with others?

8. Do you have a tendency to compete with others? Does your organization have a tendency to compete with other Republican organizations unnecessarily?

9. In what ways can you build trust with other organizations with the same or similar missions? Do you have any opportunities to collaborate with others?

10. In what ways does your organization seek feedback? In what ways can you seek feedback?

11. Considering feedback you have been given, what actions can you take to demonstrate to others that you are listening?

CHAPTER 11

Communication Style & Leadership

The discussion grew more intense by the minute. A state senator and a few longstanding members of his team argued about who they should hire to replace the chief-of-staff, who recently resigned. Rhonda, the Senator's most trusted staffer did not understand why the senator, Robert, did not want to hire Katherine.

"Katherine's record is outstanding," said Rhonda. "She has an excellent background in other offices. Her performance has been incredible. If she can't do the job, nobody can."

Robert knew that Rhonda's logic was sound, and he felt compelled to be straightforward with her. "Rhonda, I know you're right about Katherine's performance thus far," said Robert, "But if we bring her in, she will be working closely with us, and, frankly, I do not like her. It's that simple. She irritates me. She may get the job done, but from my viewpoint, Katherine is loud and pushy. I think it's only a matter of time before it affects her results. Did I tell you about the time last spring at our annual fundraiser? Why, my wife told me afterward that..."

Robert was concerned with how Katherine relates to others, which is often critical to a person's effectiveness as a leader as well as to her upward mobility in an organization. In this case, the way Katherine related to other people proved to be the primary barrier to her career move and was therefore, already affecting her results.

Performance alone does not determine who gets a job. Typically, more than one person can perform adequately in a particular role, and in such cases the deciding factor is usually related to a person's communication style. Self-awareness is essential to identifying whether your communication style is balanced. As you read about the following basic communication styles, consider whether you identify with one of them.

ASSERTIVE COMMUNICATION STYLE

The term "interpersonal relations" refers to how well a person gets along with others, makes friends, cooperates, and shows consideration for the feelings and views of others. There is a strong correlation between a person's interpersonal relations and their ability to become a strong leader. Related to a person's interpersonal relations skill is his or her level of assertiveness. To "assert" yourself is to express yourself, by making a statement or by declaring an idea, opinion or point of view. A person characterized as "assertive" is one who confidently communicates his or her interests, needs and/or concerns. People who are assertive express their opinions in situations where nonassertive people hold back.

Assertiveness is best understood by comparing it with two related behaviors: nonassertiveness and aggressiveness. Degrees of assertiveness range from non-assertive to aggressive at opposite extremes.

NON-ASSERTIVE COMMUNICATION STYLE

A person who has a non-assertive behavior can be thought of as the opposite of assertive behavior. You would be considered non-assertive if you:

- fail to stand up for yourself
- do not honestly express your interests or feelings
- are unable to do one or both of the above without experiencing undue anxiety

If you are someone who avoids conflict all of the time and who never asserts yourself, others are missing out on the perspective that you have to offer. After all, just because you are quiet does not mean you have nothing to say or to contribute. Knowing when to avoid conflict is a real skill. However, if you never address issues with which you have a problem, the issue may fester until you are far more upset than you would have been had you simply said something about it.

When people are habitually non-assertive, they run the risk of losing influence over others. Influential people are often assertive. They assert new ideas and express opinions, which help people and organizations to grow and develop. They are viewed as contributing members and are therefore valued.

On the other hand, if you are non-assertive, your teammates miss out on your point-of-view. You would not be on the team if you were not a valuable contributing member, so it is advisable to increase your use of assertiveness.

AGGRESSIVE COMMUNICATION STYLE

On the other end of the spectrum from nonassertiveness is aggressiveness. Aggressive behavior goes beyond assertiveness to somehow infringe on the rights of others. The line between assertiveness and aggressiveness is often difficult to define.

It depends, to some extent, on the situation and on the interpretation that participants or observers give the behavior. If you are aggressive, you may be at risk of experiencing the following consequences:

- Difficulty in relationships or loss of relationships
- Lack of needed feedback from others
- Reduced learning because of a lack of listening
- Surrounded by "yes people" who only tell you what you want to hear and therefore weakening of your decisions due to lack of perspective
- Lost opportunities

The situation may be the primary determiner of whether a person has a nonassertive, assertive, or aggressive communication style. For example, a parent who may be highly assertive or even aggressive in a family situation may be nonassertive at a Republican Club meeting. One's level of assertiveness is often determined by one's self-confidence and perhaps, by the degree of familiarity with one's environment.

Assertiveness depends on the situation, but it is also a relatively consistent characteristic in people. You probably know people who are shy, timid, and generally nonassertive in virtually every situation. Others, who are aggressive, can be depended upon to pick fights, to be overbearing, and inconsiderate of others. Still others, who may be described as assertive, achieve a balance. They feel comfortable expressing their points of view, confronting others when necessary, interacting with others to solve problems, and protecting themselves when attacked. Assertive people usually try not to be offensive or to tread on the rights of others, but still manage to express their opinions.

This is the balance Republicans should strike when working with each other. We must be able to work with each other and communicate our points of view respectively without being inconsiderate of others.

BENEFITS OF ASSERTIVENESS

The probability is high that when a non-assertive person adopts a more assertive communication style, their ability to lead will also increase. The following are benefits of assertiveness:

- Increase in Influence and Contribution
- Increase in Self-Confidence
- Reduction of Conflict
- Releases Inner Tension and Stress
- Increases Self-Esteem
- Shows Consideration

Increase in a Leader's Influence and Contribution

The person with the best ideas is not necessarily the one with the greatest influence. No matter how good your ideas may be, if you fail to express them, your influence and contribution will be greatly diminished. Sharing your ideas will signal to others that you are a valuable member of the team. This is particularly true when working among highly assertive or influential people. You must be assertive in order to make the contribution of which you are capable.

Max was a member of a Republican club of young professionals. He was very excited about joining the group as the election was approaching and he wanted to make a difference. After attending a few meetings he realized that there was a small group of leaders who were doing everything. While their ideas were great, he found himself seeing ways they could improve their membership development and get-out-the-vote programs. The other personalities in the group were so strong that he tended to listen quietly in meetings, rather than speak up.

Max became friends with Victoria, another member of the organization. Max and Victoria talked all of the time about politics and he began to share his ideas with her. At a meeting Victoria spoke up and said, "Max has an idea." After wincing momentarily, Max explained his idea for increasing the organization's membership. The idea was really well received and was implemented immediately. Over time, due to Max's increase in assertiveness, people began to see Max differently. He contributed good ideas that benefited the organization.

Consider each of the team members with whom you work closely. How assertive is each person? Understanding their communication styles is valuable for you to know so that you can encourage team members who are less assertive to share their perspective during meetings. Do you have team members who you can always count on to assert their opinions? Do you have team members who never assert their opinions, but who have much perspective to contribute?

Increase in Self-Confidence

Expressing your views or taking a stand on an issue helps to build the self-confidence required to take similar actions in the future. This increase in self-confidence will allow you to exercise the inner strength and courage often required to be assertive in more complicated situations.

Max discovered that he actually enjoyed sharing his ideas. It was very satisfying to see an idea through to completion. He felt like he was making a difference, which increased his self-confidence.

Reduces Conflict

Open and clear communication tends to reduce conflict. Assertive behavior creates such an environment because it is honest and healthy. In contrast, non-assertive and aggressive behaviors tend to increase conflict within an organization, among both individuals and groups. For instance, nonassertiveness can foster frustration when information seems to be lacking or when unspoken concerns are not addressed.

Miranda worked for a Congressman's home office. She loved her job and took great care of the Senator's constituents. However, there were days that Miranda felt disconnected because she did not live in Washington, D.C. On one hand, she felt like her hands-on contribution locally was most important because she had her finger on the pulse of the district. But, on the other hand, the Congressman spent most of his time in D.C. Miranda felt isolated and often like she was not a part of the team. To make matters worse, she was often inadvertently left out of important planning meetings when she believed that she had vital perspective to contribute.

Miranda never said anything to anyone because she did not want to start a conflict. However, each time she heard of another meeting her frustration built up. Then one day when she was particularly stressed out with the amount of calls she was receiving about an important piece of legislation, she learned of yet another meeting she should attend. During the meeting, one of the Congressman's aides thought that they should call the home office to ask Miranda a question because they felt she should weigh in on a matter. When Miranda picked up the phone and was asked her perspective, she blew up. "Oh, now you are calling me! I think you can figure it out for yourselves. You don't really want my opinion right now!"

The probability is high that someone like Miranda, who is normally non-assertive, will eventually express her feelings in an explosive or aggressive manner. Miranda thought that she was keeping the peace by not speaking up when in fact she was in conflict, just not acknowledging it.

This is why while it may seem counter-intuitive, assertiveness can actually reduce conflict. By expressing interests in a healthy way as they present themselves you will be much more honest and fulfilled. No one can fix a problem they do not know exists.

Reduces Inner Tensions and Stress

Being honest and up front about your interests and concerns is healthy for you and for those with whom you interact. Suppressing your feelings and failing to work out conflict may result in a variety of problems, including increased stress and frustration.

Had Miranda spoken up and shared her concerns with the D.C. office she could have spared herself stress and frustration over a period of time — stress that eventually overwhelmed her to the point where she did not feel valued by her colleagues.

Increases Self-Esteem

Think for a moment about the effect of habitual non-assertive behavior. If you are someone who never shares your opinion or ideas, how do you see yourself? How is your self-image? Is your self-esteem low? It could be, because non-assertive behavior reinforces a negative self-image. Your nonassertive behavior implies that what other people have to say is worth more than what you have to say, and consequently, that other people are worth more than you.

Nonassertiveness also implies that while other people are able to take a stand on a given issue, you cannot. Thus, nonassertiveness reinforces a self-image of weakness, lack of self-confidence, and lack of self-worth. On the other hand, if you express your ideas, you will grow stronger, be more self-confident, and feel more self-worth.

Shows Consideration and Respect

Sheila was known as a major fundraiser within Republican circles. Her magnificent home was known by many elected officials as a hot spot for raising major campaign dollars. Unfortunately, Sheila had been traveling the world and had not been home in months. So when she checked her phone messages to learn that two candidates wanted to hold "meet and greets" at her house, she was not thrilled.

Because she was so tired and was not ready to jump back into event hostessing, she did not want to have either event at her house. She immediately picked up the phone and called one of the candidates and told her the bad news. She hesitated to call the other candidate because she knew that he and his staff would be very upset and might immaturely act out. She decided to avoid this call.

For which of the candidates did Sheila have more respect? The candidate she called or did not call? Her assertiveness sent a message of respect to the candidate she called. When we freely assert our feelings or desires with others we show them consideration and respect. Sheila certainly did not do the less mature candidate a favor by keeping her feelings to herself.

Few non-assertive leaders become strong leaders. However, a leader who is over-assertive will struggle to maintain his or her influence as well. Fortunately, communication styles can be developed. If you are non-assertive you can develop your ability to communicate more often; if you are aggressive you can reduce your level of assertiveness. Finding this balance between asserting yourself, but not too much or too little, will greatly affect your ability to become a strong leader.

LEADERSHIP CHALLENGE

1. How assertive are you typically? Would you describe your communication style as non-assertive, assertive or aggressive? Why?

2. Does your level of assertiveness help or hinder your success as a leader in your Republican organization? Why?

3. Do you think that you would benefit from increasing your assertiveness, decreasing your assertiveness or keeping your assertiveness level about the same? Why?

CHAPTER 12

Adjusting Your Communication Style

Your effectiveness as a leader is linked to how well you communicate. Assertive behavior alone does not, in itself, make a person a leader, but as mentioned in the previous chapter, it is required. We reduce our long-term leadership potential when we have a non-assertive communication style or, on the other hand, an aggressive communication style.

Finding balance in your communication style is a key to building influence and often to keeping it. If you are someone who is usually non-assertive or someone who is often aggressive, there are actions that you can take that will help you to find balance in your communication style.

Interestingly, the following behaviors can help both the non-assertive person and the aggressive person to build influence. What these actions have in common is that they each communicate genuine concern for others and respect for their needs. As needed, if you set goals to increase or decrease your level of assertiveness while simultaneously implementing these behaviors, you will be more likely to find a more balanced communication style and increase your leadership effectiveness:

- Maintain and/or gain trust
- Relate with sensitivity
- Show consideration
- Shape your public image
- Be diplomatic
- Make a contribution to the lives of others

Maintain and/or Gain Trust

In order to have good relations with others, people must first trust you. Effective leadership is impossible without trust. *See the Trust Building Chapter for more information.*

Relate with Sensitivity

One of the most highly developed human potentials is our ability to empathize, to consider other people's perspectives and identify with their thoughts and feelings. When you allow yourself to assume the viewpoint of others, your sensitivities can be enhanced. There are also other ways to improve your sensitivity and interpersonal relations. The most obvious of these is learning to listen.

Authentically getting to know others in a personal way can also be extremely helpful. There is really no substitute for becoming aware of other people's backgrounds, aspirations, goals, values, special needs, and personality characteristics.

Show Consideration

Showing consideration to others is a matter of being respectful of others. It is important for Republican leaders to know and show that they value all people and what they have to offer. Leaders communicate this in the way they talk with people and how they act toward them. Character and maturity is required to show consideration for others, especially when others act aggressive and inconsiderate. Some leaders cannot do it, but those who do not react defensively, will find themselves rewarded.

Shape Your Public Image

How others see you directly affects both your leadership effectiveness and your personal success. Think for a moment about specific people you know who have a negative reputation for the following:

- talking too much
- wasting other people's time
- being unable to keep a confidence
- being constant complainers
- being impulsive

How much influence do these people have? Odds are, not very much. Unfortunately, many people with great leadership potential are held back by such reputations. Such a reputation, constantly reinforced through gossip and casual conversations, often becomes exaggerated.

Matthew was the Vice-Chairman of a Republican organization. He was often described as "impulsive" by people who knew him. Due to this label, attention was drawn to any action that Matthew took that could have possibly been interpreted as "impulsive." Once the cycle began, it persisted and ultimately kept him from becoming the President of his organization.

Reputations result from who you are and what you do. One of the best ways to improve your self-image, if needed, is to observe the actions of people you admire. Identify their strengths and then act as if you possess the attributes that produce such actions. You must intentionally set goals to break a negative perception and build a positive one. In time, others will say that you have changed, and as you become comfortable with your new behaviors you will, indeed, have changed.

Be aware of the adjectives and phrases people use to describe you in order to reverse the negatives and reinforce the positives. Consider how other people are limited or empowered by their reputations. This should help you to see how you may be seriously hurt or helped by the words people use to describe you.

Be Diplomatic

Some uniquely talented leaders develop poor interpersonal relations because they lack diplomacy. Diplomatic leaders are tactful, even during challenging situations. A diplomatic response is disagreeing without being disagreeable, compromising when the outcome is inconsequential, or using gentle language even when your feelings are strong. Someone who is diplomatic is assertive, but chooses their words wisely.

Make a Contribution to the Lives of Others

You can improve your interpersonal relations with other Republicans by making a special effort to contribute to the lives of others. We each have unique talents, access to information, and opportunities to offer. If we take note of the needs of others, rather than focusing only on our own, we will discover that the ways we can help others are abundant.

BECOMING MORE ASSERTIVE

If you are someone who is often non-assertive, you may be concerned that by becoming more assertive you will put yourself at risk of being perceived by others as behaving aggressively or defensively. It is true that becoming more assertive will involve risk on your part. However, your leadership effectiveness is likely already at risk if you do not have an assertive communication style. To develop this communication skill will require you to deliberately increase your level of assertiveness.

To guard against the perception that you are becoming aggressive, simultaneously and consistently over time, exhibit the above behaviors that demonstrate respect for the needs of others, while also gradually challenging yourself to assert yourself more.

If you begin to analyze the best of leaders you will see that they are usually highly assertive people, but they also simultaneously exhibit a genuine respect for the needs of others.

BECOMING LESS ASSERTIVE

On the other hand, if you are someone who tends to use a more aggressive communication style, the following actions will help you to improve your interpersonal relations. You already have the self-confidence to assert yourself. You understand the importance of expressing your ideas and your perspective. However, while continuing to advocate for your own interests, you should deliberately increase the amount that you express your concern for the interests of others.

By doing this, you will likely see that your level of assertiveness decreases. The positive response that you receive from others and your strengthening of relationships over time will be evidence that the changes are working.

See the Goal Setting chapter for more information.

LEADERSHIP CHALLENGE

1. Do you believe there are risks involved in increasing or decreasing your level of assertiveness? What are they?

2. Reviewing the recommendations in this chapter for how to reduce the risk in increasing your assertiveness level, are there any that you should implement?

2. If you usually behave aggressively, the recommendations in this chapter can help to decrease your level of assertiveness to a more balanced level, which will help you to maintain or build your level of influence as a leader. Are there any of these recommendations that you should implement?

3. Do you relate to others with sensitivity to their needs and concerns?

4. Do you show consideration for others no matter how they behave? In what ways do you do this?

5. What is your public image? What words would people use to describe you?

6. Do you like the words people use to describe you? Or do you need to set goals in order to change your reputation over time?

7. What steps should you take to build a more positive public image?

7. Are you diplomatic?

8. What are your unique talents and/or resources? In what ways can you help to empower others?

9. What goal(s) can you set to improve your communication skills?

SECTION 6

Conflict Management

Conflict is present when working in teams and in all organizations, particularly in politics. Even if you work among "like-minded" individuals, perspectives will vary and opinions will clash. And while conflict can be prevented to an extent, Republican leaders must learn to anticipate and manage conflict, rather than escalate or ignore it. In this chapter we will answer these questions:

- Why must Republicans manage conflict?
- What are the consequences of high conflict in an organization?
- What are common sources of conflict?
- What techniques can we use to better manage conflict?

CHAPTER 13

Why Republicans Must Manage Conflict

What do you get when you create a team of passionate people with strong opinions and ask them to fight for a common cause? There are many possible answers to this question. Some people might say, "Powerful solutions," or "change." Still others might say, "The Republican Party," or any other political party for that matter.

All of these answers are potentially true. There is one answer that is guaranteed to be true, and that is, "conflict." Yes! Even when people share passion and a common purpose, there will be conflict, because where there are two there is conflict.

Conflict can be defined as any situation in which one's concerns or desires differ from those of another person. It does not necessarily mean an argument or fight, but rather a different interest or opinion.

SOURCES OF CONFLICT

If members of a group or organization share the same mission, how can there be conflict? The bottom line answer is because we are all different. How can we not have conflict, when we are all so different? Our differences are the source of our conflicts. We have different beliefs, needs, perspectives and goals. Even the system in which we work, while the best in the world, can be a source of conflict for Republicans.

We have different religions and philosophies. Our values dictate what we believe is right and wrong. This results in different ideas about how to achieve the same end.

We all have different needs. Our needs affect how we allocate limited resources — human and financial. This becomes a source of conflict because people perceive needs differently and therefore prioritize differently. For example, two members of a Republican organization, who agree that the organization should spend money on advertising, may have different perspectives about how to budget the money during an important election year. Or a campaign manager, whose candidate has limited time, may prioritize certain events differently than the candidate.

A person's perspective is their point-of-view, or how they see the world. Two people will view life two different ways, because no two people are the same, even if they both have an "R" behind their name. This is because our perspective is based on our backgrounds, education, experience, etc.

In addition to having different values, needs and therefore perspectives, people also have different goals. People who come together with a common mission in an organization all have individual personal goals as well. People are motivated for different reasons. The clash between individual goals and those of an organization can also cause conflict.

Even the systems in place that make our country great can build in conflict that we must overcome. For example, while the Primary election cycle is one of the best attributes of our election process, it can also be one of the hardest for us to endure. Nevertheless, the Primary election is valuable and necessary. This is the voter's chance to learn about the candidates' point-of-view and how they see the world. This is when we vet our candidates and choose candidates to represent the Republican Party in the general election. However, along with this crucial process, comes a systemic hurdle that must be overcome — conflict among Republicans.

WHY REPUBLICANS MUST MANAGE CONFLICT

We know that conflict is a reality in life and in the Republican Party. We also know that the consequence of a fractured Republican Party could mean the end of the United States as we know it. So, we must win elections to preserve our country, but we will only win elections if we are unified. Therefore, even if you are coming out of a Primary election, stay focused. Do not be surprised when conflict occurs. Expect it and prepare to manage it.

The following are reasons why it is critical that Republicans manage conflict: (1) We exert more control over processes and outcomes when we resolve conflicts ourselves; (2) Our world is increasingly interdependent and so is our Party; (3) The potential consequences of high organizational conflict are destructive; and (4) Conflict can be an opportunity.

#1 — Control over Outcomes

Have you ever considered how much more control you have when a conflict first arises? Conflict is like fire. It can spread and take on a life of its own. It is important to manage conflict as it presents itself because as conflict escalates, your control over outcomes diminishes.

The simplest conflicts can grow and evolve beyond two people and become a bigger problem, unnecessarily. And the bigger the conflict becomes, the more distracting it becomes. If you are in an ongoing conflict, this could mean you are not doing critical work toward winning the election.

#2 — Interdependence

Our world is increasingly interdependent, and so is the Republican Party. As Republicans we understand very well what it means to be "independent". But, what does it mean to be "interdependent"? Try to think of anything that you have accomplished lately without depending on someone else.

Interdependence means a mutual dependency exists among people or organizations. Furthermore, there is a connection between increased levels of conflict and people who are "interdependent" with each other to complete work. Interdependent people or organizations may not have the same exact beliefs, needs or interests, but they do have interlocking interests and goals that cause them to rely on each other to be successful. With increased reliance on each other comes increased frequency of communication. An increase in communication, and a diversity of ideas represented presents more potential for conflict.

With whom are you personally interdependent to get things done? It is with these individuals or organizations that you will have increased communication, and therefore, increased potential for conflict.

Most Republican organizations are led by a President or a Chairman. This leader often works with numerous Committee Chairmen. These leaders must work together toward common goals, although their roles are different. They need each other as team members for the organization to be effective.

This interdependence requires increased communication among these members of the organization and therefore increases the potential for conflict.

Auxiliary organizations of the Republican Party often work with the party to achieve the common goal of electing Republicans. Even though each organization is independent of the other, they share a vision for America. The need for interaction between the organizations is an example of organizational interdependence. Due to this organizational interdependence, there is increased communication among the organizational leaders and therefore increased potential for conflict.

#3 — Potential Consequences of High Conflict in Organizations

Occasional minor conflicts will not necessarily hinder the success of your organization. Those are to be expected. However, you must be careful that the smallest conflicts do not grow into a consuming fire. When conflict is high in an organization, to the point where it is part of the culture, it can have a devastating effect. The following are risks associated with a high level of conflict:

- Increased Stress
- Lower Morale and Motivation Levels
- Hampered Performance
- Decreased Productivity
- High Turnover Rate
- Loss of friendships
- Potential Conflict Escalation
- Public Relations Challenges
- Violence
- Lawsuits

We absolutely cannot let conflict reach these levels in our Republican organizations. The cost is not worth the risk. Therefore, we must strive to manage conflict in our organization so that it does not spread out of control.

#4 — Positive Outcomes Can Arise from Conflict

Not surprisingly, conflict has a bad reputation. Conflict typically evokes negative feelings. This is why many people avoid conflict at all costs. And while there are good reasons to avoid conflict sometimes, if you choose to avoid conflict all of the time it can perpetuate an ongoing problem or make matters worse. So always avoiding conflict among Republicans is not the answer. There are opportunities available to Republicans when they manage conflict well. Conflict has the potential to:

- Open the door to needed communication
- Provide better understanding
- Bring about needed change
- Help restore broken relationships
- Bring about creative solutions
- Provide a process for resolving future conflicts

Leaders of a local Republican Club in a small town decided to hold a candidate forum for a congressional race during an election year. After holding a planning meeting for the event and making many decisions regarding the forum, a member discovered that the local Republican Women's Club had already asked the congressional candidates to speak at a candidate forum on the very same day. The Republican Club became frustrated because they were worried the congressional candidates would not want to come to their small town for a second forum in the same day.

To complicate matters, the Republican Club had already reserved the only facility in town large enough to host such a forum. The Republican Women discovered this when they went to reserve the building for their forum. Initially, this conflict caused a stir among the overlapping memberships of the two organizations. One Republican leader even told a member of the Republican Women's Club that the women would have to cancel their event.

However, instead of letting the conflict divide the group, the President of the Republican Club called the President of the Republican Women's Club to explore the idea of coordinating the forum together. After each leader shared the idea with their memberships, the two groups decided to work with each other. The Republican Women maintained contact with the congressional candidates and the Republican Party members kept the reservation at the local meeting facility.

Together they focused on the common interest, which was to bring candidates before the voters for a forum. Because of this conflict, the two groups found a creative solution and worked together to achieve a common goal. Co-hosting this event also brought about much needed communication between the two organizations. After the event, the organizations discovered that they had a newfound working relationship with each other, and they continued to find opportunities to work together.

This example shows how creative solutions can arise from conflict when Republicans choose to work together. Because the leaders chose to manage the conflict and explore joint possibilities, they were able to find solutions helpful to their organizations, the Republican Party and ultimately their whole community.

LEADERSHIP CHALLENGE

1. Have you ever experienced conflict when working on a team or are you experiencing this right now? What do you think was or is the main source of the problem?

2. Why is it important to you that conflicts among Republicans are managed and resolved when possible?

3. What common beliefs and goals do you share with your fellow Republicans?

4. With whom are you interdependent to be successful in your role within a Republican organization?

    a. Individuals:

    b. Organizations:

These are the people or organizations with whom you should take extra care to manage conflict well. They are important to your success and vice versa.

CHAPTER 14

Finding Win-Win Solutions

Our society values sports. We cannot get enough of it — football, basketball, soccer, you name it. We are socialized from a very young age to value and reward winners. And this is not always a bad thing. As Republicans, we recognize that competition can be a good thing. It is the basis of a sound economy. Capitalism may be imperfect, but it is the best financial system man has to offer. However, there are times to compete and there are times to collaborate. Unfortunately, we often compete with Republicans when we should be collaborating. Sometimes, even Republicans forget that they are on the same team.

A CLASSIC NEGOTIATION TALE

The "Story of the Orange" is a simple and classic negotiation tale from which Republicans can take lessons. The story has been told many ways. This is the version we were told….Two sisters were in a kitchen arguing over the last orange in the refrigerator. Their father entered to see what the commotion was all about. He discovered that his daughters both wanted the last orange, so he took out a knife and SLICE! Problem solved. He handed each daughter one half of the orange. Later, he found one of the girls squeezing the juice from the orange into a glass to drink. Her sister was grating her half of the orange, because she needed the peel for a dish she was baking.

What's wrong with this scenario? Dad assumed that the girls' interests were incompatible, just because they were in a dispute and it seemed impossible to agree. Usually, conflicts can appear this way until parties communicate with each other and discover underlying interests. Each party could have been 100% satisfied instead of 50% satisfied if someone would have just asked the question, "Why do you need it?" We assume the other side's interests are incompatible with our own, and unfortunately our results usually reflect our expectations.

OUR APPROACH AFFECTS OUR RESULTS

How can you find compatible interests among your fellow Republicans? It has much to do with how you *approach* conflict. Often people see what they expect to see. A very common approach to conflict is the "me versus you" approach. This is the competitive approach that tells us that if one of us wins, the other must lose. However, a better way to begin conflict is the "me with you" approach, and this approach can lead you to find winning solutions for all involved. Consider that you may have compatible interests with the person or organization that you are in conflict with, and you will be more likely to *see* these common interests.

BEWARE OF NEGATIVE ASSUMPTIONS

Assumptions are killers. Avoid negative assumptions about the intentions of other people or organizations. Many of us believe we are mind readers. We just "know" or have a "feeling." But this kind of thinking can be very destructive. Likewise, it is easy to imagine the worst in other people while assuming the best in ourselves. This can lead to unnecessary demonization of others. We also tend to make decisions or take action based on partial information. If we think this way, we are less likely to learn information from others or to share information that is necessary for joint problem solving. It is better to assume that there is information that you do not have. And if there is information you do not have, this means you must learn more in order to discover the truth — to see the bigger picture.

DISCOVER THEIR INTERESTS AND SHARE YOURS

If instead of making negative assumptions you signal to the other person or organization that you want to work together and find win-win solutions, the next step is to ask about their interests. What do they hope to achieve? What specifically do they need? Asking questions such as, "Why?" or "Why not?" breaks the competitive cycle and begins a dialogue. If you seek to understand the needs, desires, concerns and/or fears of others, you are likely to find that you share some needs, desires, concerns and/or fears. It is this deeper discussion about both of your actual underlying interests that will reveal your common interests and goals. Information sharing builds trust, which leads to more information sharing. The more trust you build with the other side, the more likely you are to find a mutually beneficial resolution or to work together.

Juanita decided to get involved in the Republican Party. Upon making her decision, she decided to run for Precinct Chairman. Juanita's actual goal was to maximize voter turnout. She hoped to win the election so that she could lead an effort to contact voters, block walk, phone bank and walk in her precinct. Juanita was disappointed because she did not win the election. The incumbent Precinct Chairman, Bob, beat Juanita several elections in a row. Finally, a mutual friend of Bob and Juanita asked her, "Why do you continue to run against Bob, even though he beats you every time?" Juanita replied, "All I want to do is get the voters out." The mutual friend asked, "Don't you want to be an election judge, too?" Juanita said, "No. I just want to be a Precinct Chairman." She clarified that you do not have to be one to be the other. The mutual friend told Bob what Juanita said, to which he replied, "Really? I thought you had to be a Precinct Chairman to be an Election Judge. The only reason I run for this job is to be an election judge."

Conflict between these two Republicans occurred for years without either person talking with the other about their shared concerns and different interests. Due to this bit of newly shared information, Bob did not run for Precinct Chairman again and he gave his support to Juanita. Bob became an Election Judge. Both activists were able to achieve what they wanted.

Just like in the Story of the Orange, Bob and Juanita negatively assumed that their interests were the same. They never talked with each other, which led to a win-lose scenario year after year. It was not until someone asked the question, "Why?" that the competitive cycle was broken, and Bob and Juanita were able to find a win-win solution that was available to them all along. This simple question allowed information to be shared.

How you approach conflict affects your results. If you believe that you will find common ground and set out to find it, you are more likely to find it. By approaching conflict in this way among Republicans, you will be more likely to find win-win solutions in your Republican organizations.

LEADERSHIP CHALLENGE

1. Do you ever find yourself competing with another Republican instead of supporting him or her, even when you have the same goal?

2. What opportunities are there for you to approach these situations with a "me with you" mentality instead of a "me versus you" mentality? How can you signal a willingness to support or to work with another person?

3. Has your Republican organization or group ever competed against another Republican organization instead of supporting it, even when it has a similar goal?

4. What opportunities might result from your organization approaching these situations with an "us with them" mentality instead of an "us versus them" mentality? How can your organization signal willingness to support or work with other organizations?

5. Have you ever experienced a conflict in your role within a Republican organization? If so, what assumptions did you have at the outset of a conflict? How did these assumptions affect your actions?

6. What goal can you set to help find win-win solutions in the future?

CHAPTER 15

Conflict Management Tips & Techniques

When thinking on an issue as big as "party unity", it is easier to see how "they" are the problem. It seems like only the "powers that be" have an impact on this issue. It is harder to see how we can make a difference in our day to day interactions with one another. However, party unity does begin with us, the leaders of our organization. How we manage each moment has an effect on our organization, the Party and therefore our communities.

This is why you must strive to handle conflicts in a way that you can be proud of and know that you did your best. Unfortunately, there are no guarantees that your best efforts will bring about positive outcomes or solutions. But most of the time, *how* conflict is handled has an effect on your results. The following tips and techniques, if implemented, will help you to manage conflict.

REMAIN CALM

When in conflict be sure to remain calm. Speak at a calm, steady rate and do not raise your voice. You can often de-escalate emotions by speaking slower and at the same tone or in a slightly quieter tone. Never raise your voice to speak as loudly as or louder than the other person. This typically has a disarming effect that others do not expect.

LISTEN AUTHENTICALLY AND ACTIVELY

Let people vent frustrations. Venting can be therapeutic. Oftentimes people just want to feel heard. Also, people are more likely to hear you out if you listen to them first. So, if you really want to share your perspective, note that by listening to their side of the story first it will increase receptivity to hearing your side of the story. Listening requires remaining silent, focusing on the speaker, and avoiding interrupting. Make sure the environment is conducive to a quality conversation. Move away from distractions if need be. The following actions help the other person to know that you are listening:

- Make and keep eye contact
- Lean slightly toward the person
- Nod your head as if you understand
- Listen for details
- Focus on what is being said and how it is being said
- Do not offer advice, give suggestions or talk about your own experiences or feelings

It is human nature that when our perspective is recognized by others we become more attentive, sympathetic, understanding and appreciative of other people's ideas and perspectives. In other words, when we feel heard, we are more likely to listen.

ACKNOWLEDGE DIFFERENT PERSPECTIVES

Contrary to popular belief, to acknowledge someone's perspective does not mean we *agree* with someone's perspective. There seems to be this belief that if you listen to someone else's perspective you must somehow abandon your own point of view. This is not true. There is a way to neutrally acknowledge someone else's perspective without agreeing with him or her. Acknowledgement is a neutral summarization of feelings, ideas, actions or emotional displays. Acknowledgement is not judgment. Here are some example comments that neutrally acknowledge another's perspective:

- "It sounds like you believe x."
- "It sounds like you have some reservations about us moving forward with this idea."
- "It seems like you dislike this idea."
- "It seems as if you have some concerns about what you've just heard."

SEEK BETTER UNDERSTANDING BY CLARIFYING

Clarification requests that a person go into more detail regarding his or her issue or idea. It helps you to understand and also to assist the other person in organizing his or her thoughts, if need be. Have you ever presented a new idea during a meeting only to hear the "thud" of a comment that sounds something like this, "Well, we never did things like this before…." A comment like this can be a real interruption to the flow of a meeting or even the flow of progress.

However, this person is distracted by some bit of knowledge that he or she brings to the table. He or she will continue to be distracted until his or her perspective is acknowledged. So, you may actually save time by asking a clarifying question in that moment in order to keep the conversation alive. When the person clarifies their concern, they may provide valuable information that can keep you from making a mistake or that can make your new idea even better.

Asking questions may help you uncover faulty assumptions or uncover opportunities to collaborate around shared underlying interests. Below are example responses that seek to clarify meaning and respectfully acknowledge another's perspective:

- "What specifically concerns you about this idea?"
- "What about the idea as presented wouldn't work?"
- "Have you seen this kind of thing before? What did you experience when you tried it before? Would it be possible for us to try it a different way that could work?"
- "Am I hearing you say that…?"
- "When you say "x", what specifically do you mean?"
- "Why specifically are you upset?"

There will always be new ideas. There will always be some push back. This is to be expected. Ultimately, leaders should welcome a variety of perspectives, because it only enhances their decision-making ability. Republicans must innovate in order to compete and to grow.

But, we must also recognize and value our sources of agreement and strength. We can do this by listening, clarifying, seeking to understand what we do not see and acknowledging others' perspectives.

SEARCH FOR OPPORTUNITIES TO MOVE FORWARD FROM THE ISSUE

Another option is to search for possibilities to move forward from the idea, particularly if discussion has been exhausted on the matter and you need to move on. This offers a person or group the opportunity to make deliberate choices and to determine if the negative concerns expressed outweigh the need to move forward with an idea.

In searching for options for moving forward from the situation or disagreement, our aim is to keep ourselves and others on track, working toward common goals through effective communication and action. Above all things, we need to make sure that we don't lose sight of the goals. You do not want to sound like you are hurrying someone along, because they will feel as though you are not hearing them. But, eventually, by leading the conversation toward a search for solutions, you will transition the conversation to a problem-solving mode.

- "Considering our goal, what needs to happen next?"
- "What needs to happen for us to be able to move forward from this point?"
- "Where do we agree and how can we build on these agreements to move forward?"
- "Where do we go from here? Is there something we could do that would help us get back to work together so that we can win this election?"

DEMONSTRATE FAIRNESS BY SEEKING NEUTRAL FEEDBACK

When you are problem solving in a group and two strong perspectives emerge, it can feel like there is no way to solve the problem. Many times, the two groups dig deeper into their positions and will not budge. How can you dig yourself and others out? It can help to brainstorm neutral third-party people, organizations or resources that can aid you in your decision making.

When we were kids it was easy to resolve conflicts on the playground. We would ask a teacher or adult to help resolve the conflict. When we get older and the issues are more complex, we are often the experts or appropriate authorities. But, in the same spirit of fairness, inviting a neutral third-party person, organization or resource to offer an additional perspective can help you make a decision. Sometimes it is easier to agree on this than the ultimate solution.

Brainstorm & Find Mutually Acceptable Solutions

Strive to find a solution that will satisfy the interests of both people. Include the other person in the process of problem solving. A principle to remember is that involvement usually translates into ownership. People will likely be more committed to moving forward if they helped discover the solution and they will be more likely to stand by it as well.

Develop an Effective Personal Policy

Make it a personal policy to speak and act in a way that is virtuous and honorable to you and your organization, no matter how other people conduct themselves. There is very little we can control in life. How we respond to challenging people and situations is one of them. If your handling of conflict were seen on television or on the internet would you be proud of it? Would it serve your organization or hurt it?

People have a tendency to deal differently with those they will see again. For example, imagine you are attempting to sell your car to a car salesman at a dealership. Of course you are going to try to get the best deal you can. But how would you act? Would you misrepresent or exaggerate the facts to get what you want? Would you insult the salesperson and storm out of the dealership if you do not get your way? Would you act differently if you were trying to sell the same car to your neighbor? Or to your grandmother?

No matter how you responded, there would likely be a difference between the way you would behave with the car dealer, your neighbor and your grandmother. Why is this? Relationship. We all tend to be more competitive and "burn a bridge" when we think we will never see a person again.

However, there is a funny thing about life, and politics particularly. And that is that "it's a small world." Just when you think you will never see someone again, you will see them again. Whether you are a grassroots activist, an elected official or a candidate, does not matter. What if you stormed out of the car dealership and the very next day you approached a home while working on a campaign and discovered the person's home you are visiting is that of the car dealer? Oops. Is that person going to support your candidate?

It is imperative that you act in ways that you would be proud of, not only because it is the right thing to do, but because you are a face of the Republican Party and we have a mission we must accomplish. How we manage conflict matters in the bigger picture. If we perpetuate or escalate conflict we simply waste time we could spend doing something constructive toward preserving this country.

LEADERSHIP CHALLENGE

1. Are you currently involved in a conflict? If not, consider a conflict that you experienced recently.

2. How did you respond to this conflict? Are you someone that remains calm when you have a different interest or opinion than someone else in your organization?

3. When dealing with the conflict did you listen to the other person authentically and actively? How did you approach the other person? Did you listen to their perspective? If so, how did you signal to the other person that you were listening?

4. How can you acknowledge the other person's perspective without necessarily agreeing with it?

5. How can you seek clarification of the other person's perspective?

6. What can you say to help move forward from the conflict?

7. What neutral third-party person, organization or resource is available to help you find neutral ideas or solutions when needed?

8. Which tips and techniques are most likely to help you manage conflict better in your own Republican organization?

SECTION 7

Goal Setting

Goal setting is critically important to leadership development. Leaders who plan for development position themselves to take initiative and act with a sense of purpose and self-determination. The following chapters will answer these questions:

- What are the benefits of goal setting?
- What rewards can come from setting specific leadership development goals?
- What are the common barriers to leadership development?
- How can you set effective goals that are attainable and beneficial?

CHAPTER 16

Benefits of Goal Setting

"Good ole' Betty! You haven't changed one bit since we worked together ten years ago!" Betty smiled and laughed back but then thought, "Wait a minute…was that a compliment or a critique?" Unfortunately, Betty may never know. It could have been a compliment, but if Betty is a leader, it may not have been. Her friend could have meant that Betty has not developed as a leader, and Betty is doing and saying the same things she said ten years ago, which is usually not a positive trait for a leader.

BENEFITS OF GOAL SETTING

Great leaders develop over the years. They are committed to leadership development because they understand that there is a connection between a leader's actions and an organization's results. The better a leader's skills and strategies, the better he or she will accomplish their goals. The following are among the benefits that most often result from personal goal setting:

Goals Give a Sense of Direction

People with a strong sense of direction are more likely to feel optimistic and confident. Goal-directed people have higher self-esteem than others because they have a sense of accomplishment. In contrast, people with no sense of direction or purpose feel that their work is meaningless. Feeling meaningless reflects and can produce pessimism and cynicism.

Goals Increase Our Motivation

Goals increase motivation. When we set goals we inherently accomplish more. And when we set goals for our teams, our teams are more productive. In general, people love a good challenge.

With only a few days remaining to campaign, the campaign headquarters was full of people phone banking. Almost every phone was being used. However, many of the volunteers knew each other from local Republican organizations and enjoyed seeing one another.

With the election just days away there was so much to talk about. Tom, who organized the phone banking effort, noticed that the volunteers stopped working in between calls to discuss the day's controversial editorial in the newspaper. He asked himself what he could do to motivate them to focus on their calls. He remembered that he learned how motivating goals can be and decided to post a daily goal on a dry-erase board that all of the volunteers could see. He made an announcement to the group as he wrote the target number of phone calls on the board and he also posted the number of calls that had been made already. He informed the group that he would change the number of calls made per hour.

A number of the volunteers looked up from their phones or their conversations to see Tom write the numbers on the board.

The effect of this visual goal sparked the competitive spirit in the volunteers. It caused the volunteers to behave as though they were in a race. They even began to compete with each other, tallying their own calls and showing their friends. Tom was very proud to see the motivating effect of the goal he posted. He jumped over to an open phone and began making phone calls himself.

Goals Improve Decisions

The more clearly we know where we are going and what is important to us, the easier it is to make the many small decisions that determine our everyday activities.

A campaign manager, Tom, only had a couple of days before the election. Tom felt very overwhelmed because there was still so much work to be done. Thankfully, Tom had campaign activity goals that he set at a campaign management school. According to his goals, during this time frame the campaign needed to prioritize calling as many Republicans per day as possible in order to get out the vote. The campaign workers also needed direction when they arrived at the office because they were accustomed to working on a range of activities. When volunteers showed up at the campaign headquarters and asked Tom what they should do, he told them to focus on phone calling. Having a goal to reach a certain number of Republican voters within the next two days improved Tom's decision-making ability. Without the goal he would not have known how to best prioritize tasks.

Goals Concentrate Our Energies

We live in a busy world. If we lack a sense of direction, our physical and psychological energies are scattered to the point that we are often ineffective in all of the diverse things that we do. The more focused our energies, the more powerful our impact.

Karla, a Republican activist and community volunteer, filled her days volunteering throughout her community. She was torn between participating in two upcoming events that would occur on the same day. One event was a "Get out the Vote" event for her favorite candidate and the other was a four-mile Fun Run/Walk event for heart disease.

Ultimately, Karla determined that even though both causes were worthy, noble causes, she would have to make a decision based on her own personal goals. The election was one week away and her real focus over the past several months had been working on political campaigns in order to elect candidates who agreed with her values. She determined that by staying focused, she would have a maximum impact on the results of the campaign. She chose to spend that day at the "Get out the Vote" event, where she would block walk for four miles.

Goals Improve the Quality of Leadership

Have you ever noticed how many followers a leader with an intense sense of purpose attracts, even when the leader's values and judgment are weak? It works for the leader of a street gang and even the dictator. It also works for volunteers and paid leaders at all levels of an organization, particularly those whose values are good and whose judgment is sound.

People submit themselves to the influence of goal-oriented leaders because they themselves need direction and recognize its importance in their lives.

Goals Increase Self-Confidence

We are more confident when we have a direction than when we are unfocused and indecisive. Goals reinforce our values, character and leadership practices, which increases our self-confidence.

GOAL SETTING FOR LEADERSHIP DEVELOPMENT

There are additional rewards that come from setting goals for the purpose of leadership development specifically. Leadership development will help you relate more confidently to the people around you, at home, work and in politics.

It also provides valuable insights that can guide you into future experiences that will maximize your opportunities to become a more effective leader. The greatest contribution to your life will be the potential it offers for helping you to recognize, take advantage of and interpret your future growth opportunities.

The rewards for improving your leadership performance can be many. The following are among these rewards:

- Significant contributions to causes and goals
- Increased satisfaction from the work itself
- Recognition that usually accompanies high performance in leadership positions
- Virtually limitless opportunities for advancement
- Maximum control over outcomes
- Expanded influence in the lives of others

One of the objectives of this book is to empower you with leadership skills that will help you to more confidently pursue activism, specifically within the Republican Party. Give some thought to why you want to become a more effective leader. The more clearly you can visualize your rewards, the more motivated you will be. The benefits you will receive are directly related to what you do with the information and insights you gain from reading this book.

The world is your true classroom. No discussion or activity will communicate as clearly what it takes to lead as the actions of leaders you have an opportunity to observe every day. This book can help you to learn what to look for and how to model your own leadership behavior after the best of what you see.

Developing leadership skills and knowledge is a journey. The skills and knowledge contained in this book can be helpful as a foundation for your development, but we all have much to learn about leadership.

Thankfully, you are not on this journey alone; you can learn from others who are on a similar path to realizing their potential. The actions you take and the decisions you make will certainly impact not only the Republican organization, but ultimately the fabric of our nation.

LEADERSHIP CHALLENGE

1. What benefits would you receive if you set goals for your leadership development?

2. What advantage would your organization have if you and others set leadership development goals?

3. What benefits do the causes of the Republican Party stand to gain if you and others in your organization set leadership development goals?

CHAPTER 17

Barriers to Leadership Development

Even though there are many benefits to leadership development, such as a better sense of direction, improved decision making and increased motivation, many of us do not prioritize our development. If there are so many advantages to us as individuals and to the organizations we serve that are fighting to preserve our freedoms, why do we not develop our skills?

For the same reasons that Democrats do not. We are human. There are numerous mental traps to which all of us can fall prey, and these mental traps can become barriers to our growth and development.

Fear of Change

Fear of change is a common obstacle to growth and development. After all, change can be scary. Oftentimes, even though the benefits would be great, they are not worth the stress that change would bring about.

Melvin was a veteran Republican activist. Recently, a consultant visited his political action committee (PAC) as a guest speaker and provided statistics on how much the club could increase its fund raising efforts if it allowed members to donate money online. When the idea was suggested at a subsequent meeting, it was rejected immediately. Several of the members expressed fear of providing or accepting personal information on the Internet. Others were concerned about PAC rules because of the amount of information that is needed from donors upon the receipt of a donation. Melvin reminded the members that the consultant showed them how to accept payment online lawfully and ethically by having required fields filled out before payment would be transferred. One of the members said, "We never did things that way before. And we don't need it now." When the group heard this comment, they all agreed and the conversation ceased.

In this example, the group struggled with the fear of the unknown or the fear of change. Even though there were ways to make the change lawfully and ethically, the group was not ready to make the change. Fear of change is a very real obstacle to both personal and organizational development. We are more comfortable when we work with what we know, because change can feel risky. The key for leaders is to recognize when the risk is worth the reward.

Not Understanding the Value of Leadership Development

Unfortunately, there are many people who do not understand the value of leadership development. They simply may not know what it can do for them as individuals, much less for the organizations that they serve.

Leonard was a member of the state Republican executive committee. He had served in the party for over thirty years. He prided himself on doing all of his committee's work himself. Leonard feared that if his committee members had to do work they might not want to serve on his committee anymore. Leonard was a Republican who did not understand how leadership development could help him. He was taught that people were either born leaders or they were not. No amount of training could change one's leadership abilities. One afternoon a training seminar on the topic of delegation was held as a part of his normal meeting. Leonard was so surprised by how much practical information he took away from this training session.

He realized that he had not delegated enough to his committee members. He discovered that by honing this leadership skill he could achieve so much more than he had so far, and he would likely increase the motivation of his committee members. Because of this training, he was able to put new delegation techniques into practice immediately. This changed Leonard's perspective about the value of leadership development. Because of the way Leonard's leadership behavior changed and benefited him, he learned that leadership skills can truly be developed.

BELIEVING THAT EXPERIENCE IS THE ONLY AND BEST TEACHER

Maggie had been a Republican political consultant for many years. Recently she had a client who was running for state representative. Concerned that his boss was already behind with the latest social networking techniques, the candidate's campaign manager asked Maggie to help the campaign to set up a Facebook and a Twitter account.

The campaign manager also asked if he should go to a social networking training in order to learn the latest techniques for reaching potential voters. Maggie told the campaign manager that these were just fads and that the campaign did not need these types of marketing strategies to connect with potential voters.

She also told the campaign manager that he did not need to worry himself with any kind of training because only more years of experience would help him. "You are in good hands," she said. "My experience consulting campaigns goes back so many years. Trust me, I know exactly what you need to do to win."

Fear of change, not understanding the value of leadership development and believing that experience is the only and best teacher are three very common reasons why people do not continually develop. Other reasons why people may not set goals and develop continually are as follows:

- Lack of time
- No curiosity or thirst for learning
- Only respecting information that is immediately usable and perceiving leadership development training to be impractical

Unfortunately for many Republicans, they are missing out on opportunities to grow and develop that could not only help them both personally and professionally, but also in their pursuit to effect change in this country. In order to effect change, we must be able to work with others, and leadership skills can help us do just this.

INCREASING YOUR MOTIVATION FOR LEADERSHIP DEVELOPMENT

We have probably all fallen prey to one of these mental traps. Learning more about the potential of leadership development can help us to overcome each trap. One way to stay growth oriented and keep it positive, enjoyable and unlike work, is to think of the process of growth as a goal itself. If continual movement toward a planned goal is also a goal, it can be easier to maintain high aspirations without becoming frustrated if the journey takes longer than expected.

If we believe that personal development is a life-long endeavor, even long-term goals can be continually satisfying. This perspective can provide ongoing positive reinforcement that keeps our motivation high.

LEADERSHIP CHALLENGE

1. Are there barriers to leadership development that you currently face? If so, what are they?

2. How do obstacles to your development or to the development of others in your Republican organization potentially affect your organization?

3. How can barriers to leadership development affect the causes of the Republican Party?

CHAPTER 18

Understanding How to Effectively Set Goals

All goals are not created equal. When you set goals, you should analyze them to make sure they are worth your time. Regardless of the goal(s) you set (personal, political or professional) the following steps are useful for evaluating the quality of the goal(s).

- Choose a goal that is very important to you. This will ensure that your goal is motivational and beneficial to you.

- Rewrite your goal(s) as specifically and measurably as possible. Many times goals are too vague. Ask yourself if you can measure your goal. If you cannot, clarify the goal so that it is clear to you when you have completed your goal.

- Analyze each goal to determine (1) whether it is attainable, and (2) what the costs to you will be.

- Ask yourself what personal barriers are involved? (These barriers are within you, for example your motivation, education, training, energy, personality characteristics, leadership skills, self-confidence, conflicting values, stress tolerance, etc.)

- Consider what environmental barriers are involved. (These barriers are external forces that are out of your control, for example the culture in which you live or the attitudes of leaders in your organization or having limited resources such as money, etc.)

- Determine what conflict barriers you might face. (Conflict barriers exist when you want to achieve two goals that appear to be in competition or conflict with each other).

- Consider whether it is possible for you to overcome each barrier: personal, environmental and conflict. Develop a strategy for overcoming each obstacle.

- Brainstorm the benefits you will gain from reaching your goals.

- Are the benefits worth the cost?

- Make a firm commitment to achieve the goal by a certain date or drop the potential goal. Goals without deadlines are usually not motivational.

- Decide on ways you will reward yourself for achieving the sub-goals and/or for movement toward them.

- Take action to get started on accomplishing your goal. Oftentimes, getting started is the hardest part. However, you can do it! Become a list maker! Begin each day by planning what you will need to achieve in order to stay on course. Make it happen!

Irene was a very unassertive member of a Republican Club. She had been a consistent member of her local club for years. However, Irene had never been asked to take on a leadership role in the club, nor had she expressed interest in being more involved. Also, Irene did not want to offend anyone, but she felt as though she had a lot of new ideas about how the organization could be run more effectively. Her fear of angering long-standing members of the club led her to be a non-contributing member of the organization.

Irene attended a goal setting seminar and identified that she wanted to become more influential in her political party, so she decided to set a goal to work on this. She utilized the goal setting program she was given at the seminar to evaluate her goal. Below is how Irene answered questions on her goal setting program:

IRENE'S GOAL SETTING PROGRAM

- Choose a goal that is very important to you.

  I want to be more influential in the Republican Party because I believe it is the party of freedom. I want to make a difference. However, I will need to be more assertive to do this. Right now, I never say anything. No one knows how passionate I am about the issues.

- Rewrite your goal(s) as specifically and measurably as possible. You should clarify the goal so that it is clear to you when you completed your goal.

  I will speak up at Republican meetings in order to contribute ideas or opinions. When I know of ways to get involved, I will volunteer. This way I will be perceived as someone who cares about the organ-

ization and as a contributing member. I will be more likely to be viewed as someone who could be in a leadership role someday.

- Analyze your goal to determine (1) whether it is attainable, and (2) what the costs to you will be.

- What personal barriers are involved? (These barriers are within you, for example your motivation, education, training, energy, personality characteristics, leadership skills, self-confidence, conflicting values, stress tolerance, etc.)

  My self-confidence is lower than I would like for it to be because I do not have much communication or leadership — skills training as I would like. This causes me to not speak up or take on roles that may require me to speak in front of groups.

- What environmental barriers are involved? (These barriers are external forces that are out of your control, for example the culture in which you live or the attitudes of leaders in your organization or having limited resources such as money, etc.)

  I feel as though I am in a very established organization where there are people who have been serving for a very long time. Whether it is intentional or not, sometimes I feel like it is impossible to break into the group or to make changes on how things are done. I have observed on many occasions that people feel threatened by new people and new ideas.

- What conflict barriers are involved? (Conflict barriers exist when you want to achieve two goals that appear to be in competition or conflict with each other.)

  I want to work alongside the people who have been serving in the Republican Party for years. I want to learn from them. I want to continue do the things that work well in this organization and respect the people who are currently in leadership roles. I want this to be understood, but I also want to have more of a voice. I want to see change.

- How will you overcome each barrier: personal, environmental and conflict?

    Personal Barrier: I am going to begin reading and studying leadership skills that I can put into practice.

    Environmental Barrier: I will continue to show respect for our leaders and for the action plans that work well, but I will also be persistent in my goal. I will simultaneously try to be a positive voice for change within the party when it seems like there are newer, better ways to achieve our goals.

    Conflict Barrier: When I want to assert myself, I will strive to show respect for the current leaders and their ideas before I give my ideas or opinions. For example, I can ask respectfully if I can share an idea. I can listen to their ideas before I submit mine. I can compliment someone for an idea already suggested and then add mine. "I like what you said about 'x'. What about this idea? I just wanted to consider another way of looking at it."

- Now that you have considered the barriers, is your goal reachable? At what cost? (Keep in mind the different kinds of costs: money, time, health, personal conflict, opportunities lost because of the time and/or money investment you will make to reach the goal, etc.)

    Yes, I do believe the goal is reachable. I may be perceived as too assertive at times, but I will try to build trust and respect in other ways simultaneously so that the established leaders will be more likely to listen to me.

- What benefits will you receive from reaching your goal?

  - *A voice in decision making*
  - *Possibly affect policy*
  - *I will gain self-confidence and personal satisfaction*
  - *My ability to be more influential in the future will increase*
  - *I may begin to be seen as someone who has something to contribute to the team*
  - *I will be a contributing member of the Republican party and therefore to the cause of freedom in our country*

- Are the benefits to you greater than the costs?

  Yes.

- Make a firm commitment to achieve the goal by a certain date or drop the potential goal. Goals without deadlines are usually not motivational.

  I will speak up and offer an idea or opinion at next month's meeting on December 18th.

- Decide on ways you will reward yourself for achieving the sub-goals and/or for movement toward them.

  I will turn off the TV and get out of the house. I will ask current and new friends to coffee or dessert for an evening. I could use some leisurely nights free from house work and the liberal news media.

LEADERSHIP CHALLENGE
EFFECTIVE GOAL SETTING PROGRAM

1. Choose a goal that is very important to you.

2. Rewrite your goal(s) as specifically and measurably as possible. You should clarify the goal so that it is clear to you when you completed your goal.

3. Analyze each possible goal to determine (1) whether it is attainable, and (2) what the costs to you will be.

- What personal barriers are involved? (These barriers are within you, for example your motivation, education, training, energy, personality characteristics, leadership skills, self-confidence, conflicting values, stress tolerance, etc.)

- What environmental barriers are involved? (These barriers are external forces that are out of your control, for example the culture in which you live or the attitudes of leaders in your organization or having limited resources such as money, etc.)

- What conflict barriers are involved? (Conflict barriers exist when you want to achieve two goals that appear to be in competition or conflict with each other).

- How will you overcome each barrier? (This can take time but it is well worth it. It leads directly into the next question.)

- Personal barrier:

- Environmental barrier:

- Conflict barrier:

4. Now that you have considered the barriers, is your goal reachable? At what cost? (Keep in mind the different kinds of costs: money, time, health, personal conflict, opportunities lost because of the time and/or money investment you will make to reach the goal, etc.)

5. What benefits will you receive from reaching your goal?

6. Are the benefits to you greater than the costs?

7. Make a firm commitment to achieve the goal by a certain date or drop the potential goal. Goals without deadlines are usually not motivational.

8. Decide on ways you will reward yourself for achieving the sub-goals and/or for movement toward them.

See the appendix for Specific Action Planning tools.

SECTION 8

Appendix

PHASES OF TEAM DEVELOPMENT

Phase 1: Forming: A Team is Created. During this phase, there is typically excitement about a new project or undertaking. There is also uncertainty about the expectations of the team. Team members wonder what they will do. They will question a project's importance. How can a leader help a team move beyond this phase more efficiently?

- Clarify the task or goal
- Encourage team members to get to know each other
- Ensure that expectations are clarified
- Explain the specific roles and responsibilities of team members

Phase 2: Storming: Obstacles Emerge. Conflict is common during this phase. Team members often feel discouragement and frustration. Team members question whether the project is possible or whether the goal is attainable. During this phase, team members often become concerned that conflict or other barriers cannot be overcome. How can a leader help a team move beyond this phase more efficiently?

- Remind team this is a normal phase that the team will get through
- Seek to remove barriers to success
- Remind the team of the importance of the goal

- Discuss the importance of each role and team member to achieving success
- Ask team members to share their concerns

Phase 3: Norming: Habits are Established. Team begins to feel optimism about its ability to be successful and get the project done. Individuals begin to accept team members. Team members' questions turn from whether the goal is attainable to whether the team will be able to meet deadlines. Some team members may wonder if the problems from the "Storming" phase will re-emerge. How can a leader help a team move beyond this phase efficiently?

- Review and acknowledge progress
- Encourage sharing of information to avoid premature decisions
- Praise behaviors that are worth repeating
- Ensure accountability and follow-through for all members

Phase 4: Performing: The Team Excels. The team begins to have a sense of pride about their accomplishment. They gain confidence in their individual roles and as a group. Team members begin to think about the rewards that will come from their accomplishment. They begin to consider the future and anticipate their next challenge. What should a leader do when their team excels and reaches its goal?

- Provide recognition for results
- Assess team effectiveness and adjust for better results
- Expand goals to include new opportunities

MY DELEGATION CHECKLIST

☐ 1. Give a clear description of the task(s).
   What do you need done?
   How will you know it is complete?
   What is the criteria for success?

☐ 2. Decide how much instruction to give. Does the delegatee need complete instructions to accomplish this task or does the person have the necessary experience to develop his/her own?

☐ 3. Define the boundaries of authority. The delegatee can pursue these areas and make a decision on his/her best judgment. The delegatee should check with me concerning these issues before he/she implements decisions he/she has made.

☐ 4. Alert the delegatee to areas of concern, whether they are actual or potential problems. Examples: Vendors delivering late, machinery down time, budget constraints, "political" or work environment factors.

☐ 5. Define the resources available for the assignment. Encourage creativity. Examples: Time, people, money, materials.

☐ 6. Create a timetable. Establish deadline for completion and establish reporting times throughout the duration of the assignment.

☐ 7. Be sure to encourage questions and open discussion of the assignment and where it fits on the person's regular work flow. What is the priority of this task?

☐ 8. Let go of the control and allow the delegatee to begin the task.

MY DELEGATION CHECKLIST
WHEN SOMEONE DELEGATES A TASK TO YOU

☐ 1. Seek to understand the task to be completed. Make sure you receive a clear description of the task(s).
> What specifically needs to be done?
> How will you know when you are done?
> What is your criteria for success?

☐ 2. Consider how much instruction you need. Do you need complete instructions to accomplish this task or do you have the necessary experience to develop your own plan?

☐ 3. Seek to understand the boundaries of your authority. Are you supposed to pursue particular areas and make a decision using your best judgment? Are you supposed to check back about particular issues before you implement a decision you have made?

☐ 4. Find out whether there are any actual or potential problems involved in this project that you should know about. Examples: Vendors delivering late, machinery down time, budget constraints, "political" or work environment factors.

☐ 5. Consider what resources are available for the assignment. Where will you get the resources? Ask for what you need. Examples: Time, people, money, materials.

☐ 6. Create a timetable. Establish deadline for completion and establish reporting times throughout the duration of the assignment.

☐ 7. Be sure that you understand the priority level of this task. How should you prioritize it among your other tasks?

SPECIFIC ACTION PLANNING

To get started on your goal plan, you will need specific action steps in order to achieve your goal. Answer the following questions and then transfer your answers to a one-page document that you can post at your desk or carry with you at all times. This one-page document can serve as a constant reminder of your goal and the specific behavioral steps that will help you achieve it.

- What specific actions should you start taking?

- What specific actions should you stop?

- What specific actions should you continue?

- What specific actions should you take more often?

- What specific actions should you take less often?

SOURCES

The leadership principles explained in *Leading for Freedom: Leadership Skills for Republicans* are based on over thirty years of research and development by Dr. Clifton Williams, Ph.D., as found in leadership development programs and seminars of Leadership Trek® Corporation. The content of *Leading for Freedom: Leadership Skills for Republicans* is a derivative work written by Rachel Woods, J.D. and Toni Anne Dashiell, with permission by Leadership Trek® Corporation, owned by Rachel Woods, J.D. and Dr. Mitchell Neubert, Ph.D.

The original works from which leadership principles were drawn include: *Effective Leadership, 7th Ed.*, Leadership Trek Corporation, 2007.; *Leadership Quest: Developing Your Leadership Skills and Enhancing Your Power to Influence*, Leadership Press Inc., Dr. Clifton Williams, 1985; Leadership Survival Skills Seminar, Team Building, by Rachel Woods, J.D., Leadership Trek Corporation, 2010.; and Leadership Survival Skills Seminar, Extinguishing Every Day Fire Starters, by Rachel Woods, J.D., Leadership Trek Corporation, 2008.

INTRODUCTION

Introduction content adapted from *Leadership Quest: Developing Your Leadership Skills and Enhancing Your Power to Influence*, J. C. Williams, 1985, Leadership Press Inc. Adapted with permission.

Trust: A Foundation for Leadership & Communication that Builds Trust content adapted from *Effective Leadership, Trust Building, 7th ed.*, J. C. Williams, 2007, Leadership Systems, Inc., Copyright 2007 by Leadership Trek Corporation. Adapted with permission.

Content adapted from *Effective Leadership, Decision Making, 7th ed.*, J. C. Williams, 2007, Leadership Systems, Inc., Copyright 2007 by Leadership Trek Corporation. Adapted with permission.

MOTIVATING YOURSELF & OTHERS

Understanding Your Motivation Level and Increasing Your Own Motivation Level content adapted from *Effective Leadership, Motivation Level, 7th ed.*, J. C. Williams, 2007, Leadership Systems, Inc., Copyright 2007 by Leadership Trek Corporation. Adapted with permission.

Motivating Other Republicans content adapted from *Effective Leadership, Motivating Skills, 7th ed.*, J. C. Williams, 2007, Leadership Systems, Inc., Copyright 2007 by Leadership Trek Corporation. Adapted with permission.

DEVELOPING TEAMS OF REPUBLICANS

Phases of Team Development content adapted from *Management: Current Practices and New Directions*, Bruno Dyck and Mitchell Neubert, 2010, Cengage Publishing. Adapted with permission.

"Your Team GPS" content adapted from My Team Compass Activity, Team Building Leadership Survival Skills Seminar, Rachel Woods, 2008, Leadership Trek Corporation. Copyright 2008 by Leadership Trek Corporation. Adapted with permission.

EFFECTIVE DELEGATION

Why Republicans Must Delegate & Effective Delegation Skill Building content adapted from *Effective Leadership, Delegating, 7th ed.*, J. C. Williams, 2007, Leadership Systems, Inc., Copyright 2007 by Leadership Trek Corporation. Adapted with permission.

COMMUNICATION

Introduction to Communication content adapted from *Effective Leadership, Communication, 7th ed.*, J. C. Williams, 2007, Leadership Systems, Inc., Copyright 2007 by Leadership Trek Corporation. Adapted with permission.

Communication Styles and Leadership content adapted from *Effective Leadership, Interpersonal Relations, 7th ed.*, J. C. Williams, 2007, Leadership Systems, Inc., Copyright 2007 by Leadership Trek Corporation. Adapted with permission.

Building Influence through Effective Communication content adapted from *Effective Leadership, Assertiveness, 7th ed.*, J. C. Williams, 2007, Leadership Systems, Inc., Copyright 2007 by Leadership Trek Corporation. Adapted with permission.

CONFLICT MANAGEMENT

Conflict Management content adapted from Leadership Survival Skills Seminar, Extinguishing Every Day Fire Starters, Rachel Woods, 2008, Leadership Trek Corporation. Adapted with permission.

GOAL SETTING & ACTION PLANNING

Goal Setting & Action Planning content adapted from *Effective Leadership, Planning & Goal Setting, 7th ed.*, J. C. Williams, 2007, Leadership Systems, Inc., Copyright 2007 by Leadership Trek Corporation; and *Effective Management Seminar Series: Personal Growth*, J. C. Williams, 1985, Leadership Press Inc. Adapted with permission.

ACKNOWLEDGMENTS

Numerous people graciously contributed to the success of *Leading for Freedom: Leadership Skills for Republicans.* First and foremost, we give a heartfelt thank you to our husbands, Riley Woods and Tom Dashiell. They believed in our mission and encouraged us, even before we began writing; their ongoing support and perspective is precious to us.

Thank you to our friends and family, in whom we found a strong support team: Randy and LaJean Curtis (Rachel's parents), Karen Curnock, Edward and Carla Vallejo, Joanna Stubbs and Cynthia England.

We would especially like to thank Dr. Mitchell Neubert, the Chief Learning Officer of Leadership Trek® Corporation, for his continued insights and support of this collaborative effort.

Thanks to Brian Mast, of Pilot Communications Group, Inc., for generously taking time to advise, educate, and encourage us throughout the development of this book.

Dr. Clifton Williams, Ph.D., the great uncle of and life-long mentor to Rachel, is to be commended for the over thirty years of invaluable leadership development research and development that is poured into *Leading for Freedom: Leadership Skills for Republicans.* The principles found in his leadership programs serve as the foundation of this book.

We extend a very special thanks to U.S. Senator John Cornyn for writing the Foreword of *Leading for Freedom: Leadership Skills for Republicans,* and to other Republican leaders who have championed our mission, including: U.S. Congressman Louie Gohmert, U.S. Congressman Lamar Smith, Texas Comptroller Susan

Combs, Texas State Senator Bryan Birdwell, National Federation of Republican Women Past President Sue Lynch of Wisconsin, Former Political Director for Marco Rubio, Luke Marchant, Republican Party of Texas Vice-Chairman Melinda Fredricks, and Texas Federation of Republican Women Vice President of Legislation Elizabeth "Besa" Martin.

The Texas Federation of Republican Women had a key part in bringing us together. Our friendship and every opportunity we have to work together flows from the first day we met at a local Republican women's meeting when we identified our common enthusiasm for leadership development. For this introduction, we will always be grateful.

It is with warmest regards that we thank the original Republican women in our lives, our mothers, LaJean Curtis and Alice Colace, who, from the beginning, empowered us by teaching us to believe in ourselves and to be courageous in our actions. You have been and continue to be our fierce champions. Armed with the strength you gave us, we press on in our pursuit to preserve freedom in this exceptional nation we call home.

RACHEL WOODS

Rachel Woods is a co-author of *Leading for Freedom: Leadership Skills for Republicans*. This book is a fruit of Rachel's combined passion for leadership development and for her country. She has spent a decade empowering business leaders with practical leadership skills, specializing in the area of conflict management and negotiation. She is the Founder and CEO of Leadership Trek® Corporation, otherwise known as LTrek®, through which she has trained and consulted leaders worldwide.

Soon after she began her career as an Attorney-Mediator, Rachel served as a Mediator inside businesses and began to train and consult

business leaders in the area of conflict management. This led to an invitation to teach at the Baylor Business School, where she served as a Lecturer of Negotiation and Conflict Resolution for three years. Her experiences, combined with the influence of her great uncle and mentor, Dr. Clifton Williams, Ph.D., a leadership development author and consultant, led ultimately to a career in leadership development.

Most recently, Rachel has supported the cause of increasing women's participation in public life and the spreading of democracy throughout the world, as an author, trainer and consultant. In 2010, Rachel developed the leadership development curriculum for women seeking public office in Bosnia and Nigeria through the Women's Democracy Network (WDN), a division of the International Republican

Institute (IRI). In 2011, Rachel consulted WDN in the development of women's leadership schools to be launched in four different countries, a project of the United Nations Democracy Fund. Rachel authored the *Women's Democracy Network Women's Leadership School Trainer Manual* and trained women from Georgia, Bangladesh, Guatemala and Cameroon, who now train women in their respective countries.

Throughout her life, Rachel has been a consistent voice for the Republican Party. During college she became a political activist as a member of the Young Conservatives of Texas. It was during this time that Rachel began to gain perspective about various types of Republican organizations, by spending her spare time working at the McLennan County Republican Party, the Republican Party of Texas and at the Texas State Capital. She also was introduced to the world of political campaigns during this time, when she first worked on presidential, gubernatorial, senatorial, congressional and local campaigns. As a college student, she served as an election judge, a precinct chair and as a delegate to local Republican conventions.

Today, she continues to serve as a grassroots volunteer as the Vice President of Programs of the Texas Federation of Republican Women PAC (TFRW). Previously, she served as the TFRW Chairman of Leadership Development and the Chairman of the Women Working Together Committee. In recent years, she has presented at campaign management schools, Get-Out-the-Vote workshops and leadership trainings around the state, while maintaining a blog entitled, Republicans United, through which she provides leadership tips to fellow Republicans. Locally, she served two years as the President of McLennan County Republican Women PAC (MCRW) and continues to serve the organization today.

Rachel earned a Bachelor of Arts in Political Science from Baylor University. She earned a Juris Doctor from St. Mary's University School of Law where she also trained to be a Mediator. She completed training on how to teach negotiation in organizations at the Harvard Law School Project on Negotiation in Cambridge, MA.

Rachel's proudest achievements are her marriage to her husband Riley Woods and their two children, Jackson Riley and Reagan Victoria.

She can be followed at: www.twitter.com/RachelWoods4GOP

TONI ANNE DASHIELL

Toni Anne Dashiell is a co-author of *Leading for Freedom: Leadership Skills for Republicans.* As a grassroots Republican leader and activist she brings more than 30 years of political experience to this book. Toni Anne is a leader among leaders, who was awarded the 2009 Ronald Reagan Leadership Award by the National Federation of Republican Women (NFRW) for her distinctive performance as the President of the Texas Federation of Republican Women (TFRW). She is an empowering personality who in 2010, added women from Nigeria and Bosnia to the long list of leaders she has empowered. She traveled to Bosnia and Nigeria on behalf of the Women's Democracy Network (WDN) to train

women seeking public office in campaign management, leadership development, and communication.

Toni Anne's service as a volunteer grassroots leader dates back to 1968, when she worked on a presidential campaign as a member of Teenage Republicans. Since that time she has been a consistent leader in numerous Republican campaigns including presidential, Senatorial and Congressional, statewide, city and county races.

Her combined experiences as a grassroots leader and a leadership development trainer, have given Toni Anne's insight into developing political organizations and mobilizing teams of grassroots activists to accomplish their goals. While she was president of the TFRW, in 2008 and 2009, Toni Anne mentored 165 local club presidents by instituting monthly conference calls and implemented the use of new media tools, including e-newsletters and social networking sites. During her tenure, the TFRW membership grew to more than 10,000, and she mobilized its members to support Voter I.D. legislation, which was eventually passed by the Texas Legislature. She presented in numerous campaign management schools, Get-Out-the-Vote workshops and leadership seminars. Prior to serving as president of TFRW, she served as Vice President of Campaign Activities and First Vice President, Liaison to the Teenage Republicans and Deputy President, Region IX. It is this distinguished service that led Toni Anne to receive the Ten Most Outstanding Award from TFRW in 2011. Locally, Toni Anne has served as President, First Vice-President, and PAC Treasurer of Kendall County Republican Women and she was named the Kendall County Republican Party Volunteer of the Year in 1999.

She has also served within the Republican Party organization. Toni Anne is currently serving the as the Kendall County Republican Party Chairman in Texas and is the Liaison to Texas Republican County Chairmen Association for the TFRW. She has been elected to be a delegate to numerous Republican Party of Texas Conventions and served as a delegate to the 2004 and 2008 Republican National Conventions. She was appointed as the Texas Community Service Leader at the 2004 National Convention in New York City and organized an effort for delegates to clean up a stretch of river bank in New Jersey.

Toni Anne believes in the importance of community service. She has demonstrated this value by serving as a leader in her hometown, including the Boerne Chamber of Commerce, Government Affairs, the Boerne ISD Budget Committee and the Boerne Community Theatre. She was appointed by Lt. Governor David Dewhurst in 2011 to the Texas Prepaid Higher Education Tuition Board.

Toni Anne holds a B.A. in recreation therapy. She worked as a licensed nursing home administrator and established an Alzheimer's Day Care Center before changing careers. Currently she holds two licenses for life insurance and real estate. Together, she and her husband, Tom, are small business owners, working in both real estate and insurance. She is vice president of Thomas L. Dashiell, CLU Inc. Insurance Sales and president of Dashiell Properties, Inc., Property Management Firm.